COLLINS GEM
ANTIQUE
MARKS

a mine of information

C000183957

COLLINS GEM
CRICKET

a mine of information

COLLINS GEM
DIETING

FAT

a mine of information

COLLINS GEM
DOGS

a mine of information

COLLINS GEM
FIRST AID

a mine of information

COLLINS GEM
INTERNET

a mine of information

COLLINS GEM
PREDICTING

a mine of information

COLLINS GEM
Ready
REFERENCE

a mine of information

COLLINS GEM
SHARKS

a mine of information

COLLINS GEM
WHALES
& DOLPHINS

a mine of information

COLLINS GEM
WHISKY

a mine of information

COLLINS GEM
WORD
PROCESSING

a mine of information

COLLINS GEM
Your PC

a mine of information

COLLINS GEM

FAST BIKES

Brian Laban

HarperCollins*Publishers*

HarperCollins*Publishers*
Westerhill Road, Bishopbriggs, Glasgow G64 2QT

First published 2000

Reprint 10 9 8 7 6 5 4 3 2 1 0

© Essential Books 2000

ISBN 0 00 472482-8

Printed in Italy by Amadeus S.p.A.

Contents

Introduction

Speed is addictive, and speed on two wheels is more addictive than almost any other kind – more immediate, more at one with the elements, ultimately more dependent on a degree of skill and self-confidence than even the quickest of cars. That's at the heart of what makes fast motorcycles unique, and what has always given them a certain mystique. There's very little that's as new as we think. There were multi-cylinder bikes in the early 1900s, roadgoing race replicas in the 1920s, café racers by the dozen in the 1950s, handbuilt hybrids and superbikes in every era, even if we didn't put a name to the latter until the late 1960s when the Honda CB750 came along and rewrote the rule book. They come in all shapes and sizes: two-strokes and four-strokes, singles, twins, triples, fours and sixes, even rotaries. Some are famous for their performance, some are infamous for their manners. They couldn't all be the fastest full-stop, but every one of them has something special, and that's what this book sets out to explore.

AJS 7R Boy Racer

In 1948, with petrol rationed and new models a rarity, manufacturers faced the postwar dilemma of having to rebuild a market and re-establish reputations. In 1949, with fuel available in limited supplies for racing but with supercharging banned, AJS won the first 500cc world championship with its 'Porcupine' twin. A year earlier, in 1948, they had launched the 7R, an overhead-cam four-stroke 350cc single that went on to become one of the most successful production racers of all time. Nicknamed the 'Boy Racer', it was affordable, reliable and ultra-competitive once early problems had been addressed. It had a twin-tube frame, telescopic forks, swinging-arm rear, huge megaphone exhaust and, later, a distinctively shaped pannier tank. The bike continued to evolve over the years, with revised frames, suspension, wheels, engines

BIKE FACT   First Built 1948

The 7R's sporting career spanned two decades and hundreds of wins, notably with rider Bob McIntyre.

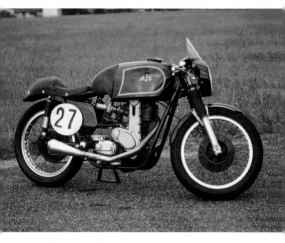

(including an only partly successful three-valve version) and gearboxes, getting quicker all the time. The first Boy Racer had 30bhp and would top 100mph; by 1951 it had 34bhp, then 37bhp; and by the end of production in 1962 it had reached 42bhp, giving 115mph, even unstreamlined. Its major race wins started with the 1952 Manx Grand Prix and the 1954 Junior TT, and amazingly continued right into the 1960s.

Aprilia RSV Mille

The RSV Mille was a long time coming between its announcement in 1995 and its launch in 1998, but it was worth waiting for. It is a classic Italian sports bike and Aprilia's first big four-stroke – a 60-degree liquid-cooled vee-twin (the only one in production in 1999), with very short stroke, dry sump, four cams, four valves and two plugs per cylinder, plus multi-point injection. Developed in partnership with Rotax, it produces 128bhp, delivered through a six-speed gearbox, and with twin counterbalance

BIKE FACT   First Built 1998

The RSV Mille was launched as the most aerodynamically efficient production bike in the world.

shafts it is impressively smooth and responsive. That gives a maximum of 166mph, but the RSV Mille isn't only about straightline speed. The engine is light and compact, and the bike is the same, weighing only around 410lb dry, with 50/50 front-to-rear distribution for exceptional stability, handling and ride comfort. The box-section double-beam aluminium frame and alloy swinging arm are closely related, in shape and materials, to Aprilia's GP racers, and are stiffer than any other production bike. The twin-disc front and single-disc rear brakes are specially made for the Mille by Brembo.

Ariel Square Four

At the 1930 Olympia Show, Ariel previewed a new engine – designed by Edward Turner, some time before his famous Triumph Speed Twin. It was a square four, in effect a pair of parallel twins, back to back in a single block, with transverse crankshafts geared together at their centres. It had overhead valves and a single overhead camshaft. In 1931 the 487cc Square Four was launched, a light, compact bike with single-tube loop frame, separate four-speed gearbox and drum brakes. It became one of the longest-running names in the business. Within a couple of years capacity was increased to 597cc, soon joined by a 997cc pushrod version, giving 36bhp in 1937. Rear-cylinder overheating and head distortion were a problem, and the inlet layout was awkward, but it was strong and flexible. In 1939, plungers replaced the solid

BIKE FACT   First Built 1931

A modified Square Four engine was used as late as the mid-1970s in the Egli-framed Healey 1000.

rear end, and in 1948 telescopics replaced girder forks. After the war, with the 600 dropped, the 1000 was updated with lighter aluminium construction, and from 1954 it gained a new head with four exhausts and 42bhp. By 1958 and the final models, 45bhp gave a top speed of 105mph. Although the Square Four was never a great handler, and grew heavier with successive models, it was always smooth, comfortable – and quick enough.

Benelli 750 Sei

Benelli had taken the four-cylinder fight to the Japanese in the early 1960s, and while Japan established the six-cylinder bike engines for racing, Benelli was first to put one into production. In 1974 it launched the Sei, a fine sight with its wide stance and six exhausts, and a natural evolution. The 748cc six, with single overhead camshaft and twelve valves, was blatantly based on the Honda 500 four, via Benelli's four-cylinder 500 Quattro. Chain primary drive took power from the centre of the crankshaft to a five-speed gearbox, awkwardly offset behind the engine. A duplex cradle frame was conventional but the details were more Italian than Japanese, and the Sei wasn't as ground-breaking as it seemed. The engine sat quite high for cornering clearance, but the Sei had decent steering and handling, and excellent

BIKE FACT   First Built 1974
Benelli did the six-cylinder production bike first; Japan did it later but better.

brakes – with twin front discs and large rear drum. It was smooth and sounded fabulous, but a claimed 71bhp wasn't the leap it might have been, even if most testers hadn't thought even that figure optimistic. Add barn-door aerodynamics and substantial weight and the Sei managed around 118mph. The later 900 would better 130mph, but so would plenty of 1970s Japanese fours.

Bimota SB4

Bimota took its name from the first letters of the surnames of Valerio Bianchi, Giuseppe Morri and Massimo Tamburini, three young designers who founded a heating equipment company in Italy's supercar and superbike belt in Rimini in 1966.

In 1973 Bimota switched to bikes, and like its supercar neighbours it hit the exclusive and expensive end of the market. Essentially, it adopted other people's engines, made its own tubular beam frames and added the best running gear, much of it specially machined and all hand-assembled. Bimota's bikes soon built a reputation for faultless handling and enhanced performance from reduced weight. The earliest were racers, but road bikes followed, beginning with the SB2 in 1977. The single-seat SB4, launched in 1983, used a near-standard Suzuki GSX1100 air-cooled four-cylinder engine giving 112bhp and a

BIKE FACT   First Built 1983

Supercar builder Lamborghini once made heating equipment, as did the superbike builder Bimota.

maximum of almost 160mph, helped by light
weight, high gearing, compact dimensions and
that excellent Bimota streamlining. The quality
of the engineering, plus details like rising rate
monoshock rear end, adjustable damping, cross-
drilled twin front and single rear disc brakes, and
low-profile radial tyres, gave the SB4 sensational
handling and braking, while retaining the image
of absolute quality and exclusivity.

Bimota DB1

In 1985, with the DB1, Bimota took an even more exclusive path than they were used to, sidestepping the entire catalogue of high-performance Japanese multi-cylinders for something from closer to home, a Ducati vee-twin. It wasn't the first time they'd used a non-Japanese engine, nor even the first time they'd used an Italian one, since some of their smaller 1970s racers were Aermacchi powered, but the combination of Bimota and Ducati was a spectacular one. The engine in question came from the Ducati Pantah, in 750cc form because the DB1 was offered as both road bike and Formula One racer. The vee-twin had Ducati's trademark desmo valvegear, with positive, cam-actuated valve closing rather than conventional springs, and for the DB1 it produced 70bhp, delivered through a five-speed gearbox for a

BIKE FACT   First Built 1985

Ducati power and Bimota chassis made the DB1 viable as both road bike and Formula One racer.

maximum of almost 135mph in the road version.
As typical as Ducati's valvegear was Bimota's
fantastic detail quality and all-enveloping
bodywork, in this case covering a complex
tubular frame with monoshock rear and using the
engine as an integral, load-bearing unit. It had a
deep-voiced character quite different from its
Japanese-engined cousins, but some things, like
the impeccable handling and the effortless
performance, were familiar Bimota territory.

Bimota YB4

In 1987 Bimota captured its biggest racing crown thus far; with the Bimota YB4 it won the Formula One TT Riders Championship. In addition to being a championship-winning racing bike the YB4 was also offered as an incredible road machine.

In road guise it went on sale in 1988. The bike that had finally beaten the Japanese at their own racing game was powered by a 749cc liquid-cooled Yamaha FZ750 in-line four engine. That already had five valves per cylinder, but for the road Bimota added fuel injection and sophisticated electronic engine management, which increased peak power from 100 to 121bhp. This gave even more low- to mid-range flexibility through the five-speed gearbox, and a quoted maximum of 165mph. Bimota's achievement in turning the YB4 into a wholly

BIKE FACT   First Built 1987
The Bimota, which took the Formula One TT Riders Championship, became a totally usable road bike.

usable, stunningly well-balanced and very forgiving road bike was most impressive.

Of course it had all the hi-tech elements of the time, including the ultra-stiff external aluminium alloy beam frame with the engine as a load-bearing element, minimal weight at only 396lb dry, and anti-dive front forks, rear monoshock and fully floating front discs – but it also had the touch of Bimota magic that lifted it up and beyond the reach of the Japanese road-bike opposition.

Bimota Bellaria

For a long time it was a Bimota trademark that
their roadgoing motorcycles had only one seat,
underlining their racing pedigree, but the
Bellaria, launched in 1990, broke with that
tradition and had room for two. It didn't mean
that Bimota were going soft and compromising.
The Bellaria (it means 'good air') was in every
other respect a classic Bimota, and although it
was a mid-sized machine by capacity and
dimensions, it was a lightweight in its instantly
responsive handling character and amazingly
crisp steering. Power came from a liquid-cooled
four-cylinder twin-cam Yamaha FZR600 engine,
tweaked by Bimota to increase output by 10bhp
to 95bhp, in a package more than 30lb lighter
than the Japanese donor. The six-speed gearbox
is also Yamaha's and not the bike's best feature,
but everything else is business as usual, from

BIKE FACT   First Built 1990

The Bellaria broke with one Bimota tradition, but it
wasn't the one about superbike performance.

classic alloy vee frame to upside-down front forks, monoshock rear and powerful perforated disc brakes. The twin-headlamp bodywork was tightly sculpted around the mechanical skeleton and digital instrument panel, and the combination of increased power, reduced weight and slick aerodynamics gave it a top speed of 150mph – this time to be enjoyed by two.

Bimota Tesi

The Tesi, launched in 1990, was something of a
rebirth for Bimota, after the company had gone
through a very difficult financial period leading to
a major restructuring in the mid-1980s, a closer
relationship with Yamaha as engine supplier for
Bimota's resumed racing and road bike
programmes, and long delays for the Tesi itself. It
was conceived in the early 1980s, before the
financial problems, as a Honda 400 four-cylinder-
engined racer, but when the Tesi 1D appeared as
a production model in 1990 it was a different
machine. This one was another classic Bimota
single-seater, powered by a 90-degree Ducati vee
twin. There was also an 851cc version but in the
usual 1D guise with a capacity of 906cc, double
overhead camshafts, desmo valvegear, four valves
per cylinder and fuel injection, the Ducati engine
delivered 113bhp through a six-speed gearbox for

BIKE FACT   First Built 1990

Conceived with a Honda engine, born with one from
Ducati, the Tesi was proof that Bimota were back.

a claimed maximum of 156mph. This time there was an all-alloy diamond frame and swinging-arm suspension at both front and rear, in both cases with monoshocks. In fact Bimota was back with a flourish of new technology, which also included integrated engine management, an adjustable frame and revolutionary hub-centre steering, which dispensed with forks and accomplished steering by rods. It was a fine return.

Bimota Tuatara

Even by Bimota's standards, the Tuatara, which joined the family in 1990, was a bomb. It was top of the range, with a price tag which swiftly made it the most expensive production motorcycle in the world. At least this was backed up by some of the most beautiful engineering in the bike world, the result being possibly the outright fastest road bike ever made. Completely handbuilt in Bimota's small Rimini factory, it was closely related to their championship-winning YB4EI racer, and powered by a fuel-injected, electronically-managed version of the Yamaha FZR1000 engine. That engine was a liquid-cooled, twin-cam, in-line four with a capacity of 989cc, and with Bimota's improved inlet and exhaust systems it gave 152bhp, which was the most that even Bimota had yet squeezed into a road bike.

But that was only the start. The target for

BIKE FACT   First Built 1990

At launch it was certainly the world's most expensive production bike, and possibly the fastest one.

the Tuatara, for a tiny number of extremely wealthy customers, was to produce World Superbike performance on the road, and that target was reached. Quoted top speed was '180mph-plus', factory testers saw as much as 187mph, and the 989cc Tuatara was little bigger and almost exactly the same weight as the 600cc Bellaria, with all the benefits of Bimota's finest frame and suspension technology.

BMW R90S

Since the early 1920s, BMW has embraced the two-cylinder, horizontally-opposed 'boxer' engine, and perhaps the greatest compliment to the breed is that although they have rarely been the most glamorous of engines, the BMW flat-twins are still going strong in the late 1990s. In 1974, the R90S was the first of the family to pass 750cc, adding performance to the unburstable tourer genes. Its 898cc pushrod engine had higher compression and larger twin Dell'Orto carburettors, boosting power to 67bhp and top speed to 125mph, in spite of a dry weight of 474lb. It was the fastest bike BMW had at that time built, and with flamboyant colour schemes it was no shrinking violet, but when compared with Japanese and Italian rivals, it was still more about comfort, refinement and quality than outright performance. With its low centre of gravity,

---

BIKE FACT   First Built 1974

First used in the 1920s, BMW's flat-twin layout is one of the industry's greatest survivors.

compliant, long-travel suspension and BMW's
first hydraulic disc brakes it actually handled and
stopped better than some Japanese
contemporaries. But with its neat handlebar-
mounted nose fairing, comfortable seat and riding
position, softer suspension, luggage-carrying
ability and new five-speed gearbox, its real
strengths were its appetite for long-range 100mph
cruising, its absolute reliability and its
thoroughbred engineering quality.

BMW R100RS

In 1976 BMW took the sportier theme created by the R90S a stage further when they created the R100S and its cousin the R100RS. As the number suggested, capacity for the ubiquitous pushrod flat-twin had increased again, this time to 980cc, but that was just the start of the story. The R100S was again the sporty model, but the RS took the sports tourer into a new generation as the first production bike with a full, factory-fitted fairing. That was designed in the Pininfarina wind tunnel, and was intended for comfort, not for speed, giving the rider superb protection from the wind and even rain, to add to the familiar ride comfort and mechanical solidity of the shaft-driven, disc-braked BMW tourer family. Power was up to 70bhp in the R100RS – actually 5bhp more than in the sportier S, but with rather more weight to move too – so the RS maintained a top speed of

BIKE FACT   First Built 1976

The R100RS was the first production bike in the world with full, factory-fitted fairing.

around 125mph. With excellent fuel consumption and an unusually large fuel tank, it had terrific range, and on the right roads it would keep up to three figures all day, with the rider snugly protected from buffeting by the clever fairing – which was also shaped for optimum high-speed stability and low noise.

BMW K1

In BMW terminology, R had always indicated the horizontally-opposed 'boxer' engine configuration; in 1983 they introduced a new configuration, prefaced by the letter K, and with it broke with sixty years of tradition. The new engines were in-line rather than horizontally-opposed, with either three or four cylinders and approximate capacities of either 750 or 1000cc, in models launched as the K75 and K100. The twin-cam engines were water-cooled, mounted with their cylinders horizontal and longitudinally rather than across the frame. They acted as a load-bearing part of the frame, with shaft-drive running through the single-sided 'Paralever' swinging arm. Having established the pattern, in 1989 BMW gave it their sportiest shot so far, in the sensational K1. This 100bhp machine had fully-faired ultra-modern looks (including a part-

BIKE FACT   First Built 1989

Four cylinders in a line rather than two across the frame re-invented the BMW sports motorcycle.

faired front wheel and a pillion seat concealed under a removable rear fairing) with flamboyant paintwork and badging, and a top speed of more than 145mph. The uprated four-pot engine had 16 valves, fuel injection and electronic management, and the K1 continued the lead of the K100 with the option of ABS for its all-disc brakes, finally giving BMW riders a real alternative to the Japanese superbike opposition.

Bridgestone 350 GTR

Nowadays, Bridgestone is best known as a tyre manufacturer, but briefly in the 1960s the Japanese company was also a motorcycle manufacturer, building one of the most technically advanced bikes of its day. Launched in 1966, the 350 GTR advertised a maximum of 110mph, 0–60mph in 5.2 seconds and a standing quarter-mile in 13.7 seconds – all figures which, as not only Bridgestone but also most contemporary road testers pointed out, would embarrass many rival 500s and quite a few 650s. It was designed without compromise. Its air-cooled parallel twin-cylinder two-stroke engine had aluminium cylinder barrels, oil injection, the first disc valves in its class and claimed an amazing 40bhp. There was a six-speed gearbox with a dry racing-type clutch, a rigid double-cradle frame, unusually large front and rear drum

BIKE FACT   First Built 1966

At its launch the 350 GTR was widely described as the most technically advanced motorcycle in the world.

brakes, and wheels balanced at the factory. It was
pretty light at 363lb, and its looks were as sporty
as its specification, with dual 'racing-type' seat
and sweeping twin exhausts. What's more, it was
untemperamental, remarkably flexible for such a
high-revving engine and had a fine blend of
comfort and sharp handling. Sadly, it lasted
barely two years before Bridgestone returned
to other priorities.

Brough Superior SS100

In the 1920s and 1930s, Brough Superior motorcycles were widely regarded as the best in the world, and advertised, with official approval, as the Rolls Royce of motorcycles. In a way they were an odd candidate for such adulation, built, as most of them were, around bought-in engines and with plenty of unconventional thinking. The most famous was the SS100, which evolved through many versions between 1925 and 1940 and from the start lived up to its badge with a guaranteed tested maximum of more than 100mph. The first had a special vee-twin JAP engine of 988cc and a claimed 45bhp in a light and stiff but fairly long-wheelbase frame with hand-lever-shifting three-speed gearbox, leading-link front forks with friction dampers, and rigid rear end. What it lacked in handling agility it made up for with great flexibility and good

BIKE FACT   First Built 1925
For all its fine engineering, the Brough is remembered as the bike on which Lawrence of Arabia was killed.

brakes, and every Brough was fully equipped with every feature a customer could desire, from speed and distance recorders to custom-made luggage panniers. From 1928 there was the option of rear suspension, and from 1933 a more modern JAP engine and a four-speed gearbox as the familiar layout was constantly updated. Every Superior SS100 also had considerable style.

BSA DBD34 Gold Star

In 1937, BSA racer Walter Handley lapped the Brooklands racetrack at over 100mph on his single-cylinder 500cc BSA Empire Star and earned the traditional Brooklands Gold Star award for his achievement. In 1938, to celebrate, BSA named their new production bike, the 'replica' of Handley's machine, the Gold Star.

It was the start of a line that ran from the 1930s right through to the 1960s, and which remains legendary to this day. The first of the line was a 496cc pushrod-valved vertical single machine that produced 30bhp and gave a top speed of around 90mph for the road. It had a cradle frame with tubular girder front forks and a solid rear.

It looked sporty and it lived up to its looks, for with its light weight and excellent handling it was well worthy of the Gold Star badge. After the

BIKE FACT   First Built 1938

Gold stars were awarded for lapping Brooklands track at a specified speed. BSA's star outlasted the circuit.

interruption of World War II, it became even
better. In 1948 it reappeared. This time round it
was as a 350cc single with telescopic-forks, later
to be joined by a 500cc version. Then, in 1956,
came the most famous of them all, the DBD34
Gold Star. It was a beautiful, sporty bike with
distinctive chrome-sided tank, swept-back
exhausts and 42bhp from its single-cylinder two-
valve 500 engine. The result was a maximum
speed of some 110mph. It is perhaps the
quintessential British bike of all time, and
certainly was one of the motorcycle icons of the
Rocker era – until production ended in 1963.

BSA Rocket 3

The Rocket 3 was BSA's last stand against the
coming of a new generation of multi-cylinder
Japanese superbikes, led by the Honda 750 Four.
Like the Honda, it was launched in 1969
alongside the Trident from sister company
Triumph (see entry on page 162), and initially
Rocket and Trident were subtly different.

From the start the Rocket 3 had its engine
inclined slightly forwards, a design the Triumph
only copied later. It had a duplex frame rather
than Triumph's single-tube, but otherwise, badges
and details apart, they were identical. The three-
cylinder was really an extension of the classic
Triumph twin, so where the Japanese moved
towards overhead camshafts and multiple valves,
the BSA had pushrods. And it still used a four-
speed gearbox, and drum brakes. It wasn't all
bad. The 741cc BSA produced 58bhp compared

BIKE FACT   First Built 1969

The triple that was actually a twin – virtually identical
to Triumph stablemate, the Trident.

to the Honda's 67, but being lighter it could match the Honda's 120mph maximum, and the Rocket 3 had the edge in roadholding and handling. It also had a distinctive and very sporty sound, and it was the basis for a very successful racing model. But good as it was in some respects, it was too little and too late, and by 1972 the BSA part of the story was over.

Buell X1 Lightning

Racer Erik Buell designed and built a 750cc square four, rotary-valve two-stroke in 1983, for road racing in America. In 1984 he built his first production RW70, just as the AMA chopped the series it was designed for. So Buell, a former Harley-Davidson engineer, planned 'the first world-class sportbike for the road designed and built in the USA'. In effect what he did in 1987 with his fisrt bike, the RR1000, was to build a sportier Harley. Buell has been doing that ever since, from 1998 owned by Harley-Davidson. But Buells are far more than a customised Harley, they are serious sports bikes built around a Buell engine built by Harley-Davidson. The 1999 X1 Lightning further develops Buell's three basic principles: a rigid frame, low unsprung weight and centralised masses. It has a short wheelbase, very upright forks, a deep cast-aluminium rear

BIKE FACT   First Built 1999
Buell is now a part of Harley-Davidson, but Eric Buell's creations still have a character of their own.

swing arm and single rear suspension unit under
the engine for maximum compactness. The all-
black, fuel-injected 1203cc vee-twin gives 95bhp,
with belt final drive. A single front disc with six-
pot calipers saves unsprung weight and with its
distinctive snaking exhaust and frame-hugging
bodywork it is America's sportiest production
bike by far.

Ducati 750 Sport

Ducati's rise was a remarkable story, restructuring in Bologna after World War II to build 50cc 'clip-on' motorised bicycle engines, moving into motorcycles proper, going racing, making ever sportier road bikes and becoming almost synonymous with 'desmo' valvegear.

In 1971 it built its first 90-degree vee-twin, the sporty 750 GT, turned it into a winning racer in the 750SS, and back into an even more aggressive road bike in 1972 with the race-replica 750 Sport. The GT had a valve-spring engine and around 60bhp, the 85bhp works racer and the 74bhp Sport had desmodromic valvegear (using cams instead of springs to close as well as open the valves) for more positive control and higher revs. The single-seat Sport, which was painted a rich yellow, was a classic café racer, with high-set footpegs, clip-on bars and swoopy, megaphone-

BIKE FACT   First Built 1972

Ducati's first vee-twin established a layout that has lasted for three decades.

shaped exhausts. Being quite light and with
minimal frontal area, it would top 130mph and
while it wasn't particularly quick off the line,
close-ratio gears gave it the most superb mid-
range performance. With its long wheelbase it
tended to be heavy at low speeds, but a low
centre of gravity and race-bred frame made it a
brilliant high-speed handler, and the real start
of the Ducati legend.

Ducati 900SS Hailwood Replica

In 1978, legendary racer Mike Hailwood came out of two-wheel retirement to take a sensational Formula One TT victory riding a privately entered, works-prepared 900 Ducati, helping Ducati to the first of many world titles. Ducati celebrated with another roadgoing race clone, the 900SS Hailwood Replica, launched in 1979 as a limited edition based on the already very desirable 900SS. That bike had grown up from the 750SS and with a capacity of 864cc gave around 75bhp for a maximum of 132mph. The leap from here to race replica wasn't a big one; the 900SS, introduced in 1975, was already one of the most uncompromising road bikes of its generation as well as being one of the quickest. It was very light and minimally equipped, with just a top fairing and without even an electric starter. Its power was very vocal, with tuned exhausts and

BIKE FACT   First Built 1979

Mike Hailwood won more TTs than any rider of his era, and gave his name to one of Ducati's classics.

big, unsilenced carburettors. It had the
impeccable handling born of a very rigid frame
using the engine as a stressed element, and
making the 900SS as close as you'd get in 1978 to
a racing bike on the road. Except for the
Hailwood Replica, which was mechanically
similar but added to the equation a full fairing
and striking red, white and green racing colours –
and, a little oddly, a dual seat.

Ducati 851 Sport

With the 851 (and under the new, more stable ownership of Cagiva) Ducati took another upward turn into the 1990s. The 851, launched in 1988, was the new basis for Ducati's ongoing assault on the World Superbike championship, and ultimately it was available in every guise from superfast road bike to off-the-shelf customer racer, or no-holds-barred works entry. Its desmo vee-twin was getting ever more sophisticated and refined, in this case with liquid cooling, four camshafts and eight valves per cylinder. In the factory racers it could deliver a remarkable 131bhp, but even in road trim it gave 105bhp and a top speed of 152mph. Again, there were other traditional Ducati advantages. Although the 851 was at least as powerful as rival Japanese multis, it was lighter and more aerodynamically compact, and with its six-speed gearbox and the basic vee-

BIKE FACT   First Built 1988

In the 1980s, Ducati almost went out of business, but the 851 brought the company back with a bang.

twin virtue of a big power spread it had
noticeably superior mid-range performance. It
had the usual steel-tube frame rather than the
increasingly fashionable alloy box beams, but
with the stressed-element engine, bimetallic disc
brakes, and fine suspension using anti-dive front
forks and adjustable monoshock rear, it was
another hard-going, hard-stopping, sharp-
handling step ahead.

Ducati 888 SP5

Ducati themselves revealed how they saw the 888
SP5: 'a perfect replica of the model that
triumphed in the world superbike
championships, the 888 SP5 is a formidable
sports machine with stupendous performance on
the track but also perfectly at its ease in road use'.
More and more as the superbike victories
mounted up and the road bikes basked in the
reflected glory, that was the Ducati mission
statement for the 1990s. But it wasn't just
advertising hype; the machinery was reaching a
sublime level. The SP5 was at the sporty end of
the 888 family. At just 414lb it was almost 31lb
lighter than the 'ordinary' 888 and with all the
promised racer genes. It had a short-stroke
liquid-cooled 888cc four valve per cylinder
'desmoquattro' vee-twin with fuel injection and
electronic ignition. It had another light and

BIKE FACT   First Built 1993

Light weight, compactness and superb detail led
Ducati into its next generation of race-replica bikes.

delicate-looking but ultra-rigid multi-tube steel
frame, in this case with adjustable, inverted front
forks and progressive rate, adjustable rear
monoshock suspension, plus floating double-disc
front brakes and fixed single rear disc brake. And
it was another winner – again in Ducati's words:
'the most authoritative representative of the
future generation of the fastest and most
powerful roadgoing supersports machines'.

Ducati Monster 900

By the time they came to starting the Monster family in the mid-1990s, Ducati could do virtually no wrong in the eyes of the motorcycle connoisseurs, and far from sitting back they were, if anything, becoming even more daring and provocative. The 900 Monster is a perfect illustration. There was no pretence of finesse, not even the usual super-sleek fairings to cover the mechanical marvels, just naked, take-no-prisoners aggression in the styling and the inevitable superbike excellence in the running gear. The lack of bodywork beyond the swoopy tank and low single-seat moulding revealed a fully triangulated multi-tubular frame with the engine as ever doing duty as the lower load carrier, and as ever the legendary desmo vee-twin, here 904cc, air-cooled (with the help of a large oil cooler), with single overhead cams and two valves per

BIKE FACT   First Built 1993

With no bodywork, the Monster introduced a fashion for leaving the technology on show.

cylinder, and two carburettors. It made the
Monster look both shorter and chunkier. The
bike was almost intimidating. It had the normal
credentials of thoroughly developed brakes,
suspension and steering, and at just 405lb it was
at the lighter end of the market, but the fact
remained that what the Monster had most of was
style and attitude. As Ducati said, 'See it – want
it: an instantaneous process.'

Ducati 996SPS

Towards the end of the 1990s, the balance
between the big twins and the multis was shifting
slightly. In the past, the multis had had the power,
the twins had had the light weight, the compact
packaging and the sharper handling. Then the
twins started to add a lot more power without
adding quite as much weight, and thereby
challenge the real-world performance of even the
fastest fours.

There was no better example than the
Ducati 996SPS, a Ducati with the outstanding
handling the marque is famous for, but with more
power than ever. The frame was the familiar
small-tube trellis with upside-down front fork and
fully adjustable monoshock rear, triple discs, 17-
inch wheels, gorgeous swoopy exhausts and
typically sleek Ducati bodywork. Power was from
a very short stroke, fuel-injected, 996cc version of

BIKE FACT   First Built 1997

Speed, sound and jaw-dropping good looks combined
to make the 996 *the* biking icon of the 1990s.

the 90-degree Ducati twin, offering a multi-chasing 132bhp. At around 425lb it was a bit heavier than its smaller stablemates, but not so much that this blunted its 167mph top speed and massive mid-range punch. And although the power delivery was inevitably less smooth than that of the fours, the handling retained that traditional Ducati edge, putting the 996SPS's overall abilities into a class of one.

Egli Vincent

Before he turned to housing large-capacity engines from BMW, Ducati and Japan, Swiss chassis designer Fritz Egli cut his teeth on their spiritual forerunner, the Vincent. He wasn't the first to reframe the big, powerful Vincent vee-twin, as plenty of Norton-Vincent builders would testify, but he was the first to build a frame specifically for the purpose, and to build it commercially. Fritz had raced Vincents and knew their handling faults, which he set out to avoid. He created a Vincent-type backbone frame, whose oversized round-section top tube contained the oil and carried top mounts for the externally unmodified

---

BIKE FACT   First Built 1968

When Fritz Egli combined Vincent vee-twin power with his own frame, he went from also-ran to race winner.

engine. He added telescopic forks, a strong swinging arm with top-quality suspension units, and mechanically-operated triple-disc brakes. Never having finished above third place before, he won every race he entered in 1968, and the Swiss championship. He put the Egli Vincent into production in the same year, in three versions – a Shadow-based fast tourer, a very quick road bike based on the Black Lightning, and a full racer, built to customer specification. His mildly tuned Shadow twin gave around 62bhp and the Lightning 73bhp, for a maximum of more than 130mph, with considerably improved handling.

Harley-Davidson WL45

In 1909, after some years building single-cylinder bikes, brothers William A, William S and Walter Harley and friend Arthur Davidson built their first vee-twin. After a slow and troublesome start, the 45-degree engine was improved to the extent that it became Harley-Davidson's core product, and a legend was born.

There have been too many famous Harleys to count, but to give a flavour, look at the 45 series. Forty-five is the capacity in cubic inches, equivalent to 742cc, to Harley a 'small' capacity. They introduced it in 1929 with side valves, in a very simple bike – and in hard times it sold well enough to help keep Harley-Davidson afloat.

In 1937 it was the foundation of the W series, the company's staple military output through World War II and basis of a new civilian line after it. The wartime WLA and WLC 45s

---

BIKE FACT   First Built 1949

The Harley-Davidson business started in what was little more than a shed, but grew to be world-famous.

introduced thousands to Harley ownership, and after the war Harley built a whole family, which included the sporty 25bhp WL45 – the archetypal entry-level Harley of the 1940s and early 1950s. Admittedly, for a book of fast bikes, it was never actually that fast, and would only just threaten 70mph, but as is the case with most Harleys, that was hardly the point.

Harley-Davidson 61E

As the capacity of 45 cubic inches meant 750 cubic centimetres, 61 cubic inches meant 1000cc, and for many decades that was a standard Harley-Davidson big-capacity number, as in the famous Series 61. The 61E was introduced in 1936, and was instantly nicknamed the Knucklehead due to the prominent shape of the rocker covers on its new overhead-valve heads with hemispherical combustion chambers – an important advance from the flathead layout of all earlier Harley models. This helped to take power up to 37bhp in the standard E, and top speed to a heady 90mph or so. To match this new-found power it had a stronger twin-tube frame, coil-sprung front fork and solid rear frame. It had a four-speed gearbox and chain drive, with front and rear drum brakes that were just about big enough for its weight and performance. It became

BIKE FACT   First Built 1936

The nickname Knucklehead aptly described Harley's first overhead-valver, and the name stuck.

a reliable and (in Harley terms) refined cruiser, and in stripped and tuned trim set many speed records, which added to the image. But its biggest asset was its looks, the teardrop tank with tank-top instrument panel, the deep-fendered mudguards, the low seating position, the long, sloping front forks. Over sixty years on, it couldn't be anything but a classic Harley.

Harley-Davidson XLCR1000

In 1957, into a range dominated by big, showy cruisers, Harley-Davidson launched a sportier machine, the XL Sportster – and in 1958 it actually became sporty, in the pared-down XLCH. While still clearly a Harley, the bike had a lower, leaner look, with straight-through exhaust pipes, small tyre-hugging mudguards rather than huge fenders and a small 'peanut' petrol tank. Harley revamped the 883cc twin of the original XL, and Sportster became a long-running range, in various capacities and degrees of sportiness.

In 1976 it gave rise to the sportiest of them all, the XLCR 'Café Racer'. The idea was simple: in the XLCR Harley put a highly-tuned, short-stroke 997cc Sportster vee-twin with 61bhp into the lighter and more compact frame of the famous XR750 flat track racer. But that was not

BIKE FACT   First Built 1976

The CR stands for 'Café Racer', and the lighter, lower XLCR was one of Harley's sportiest production bikes.

all, for the XLCR was black on black, it was low and looked mean.

Black paint, black engine casings, black siamesed exhausts, a tiny black fairing, black wheels highlighted by bare alloy rims. It looked superb. It also looked quick and, at 120mph tops, it was. For a Harley. It looked compact and it was. For a Harley. At barely 500lb it was light. For a Harley. It handled, steered and stopped superbly. For a Harley. At the time few understood it; now it's a Harley icon.

Hesketh V1000

In the mid-1970s Lord Alexander Hesketh was a flamboyant four-wheel Grand Prix team owner. By 1981 he was a motorcycle manufacturer. His aim with the Hesketh V1000, as with motor racing, was to show that Britain could match the world. He planned series production, in small numbers, in the bespoke image of predecessors like the Brough Superior and the Vincent motorcycles. The Hesketh was designed and prototypes built with few compromises and a frightening budget. The end product oozed quality, if not modernity.

The frame was a beautifully-made nickel-plated tubular perimeter carrying the best available proprietary suspension and brakes and lovely, riveted, anodised five-spoke alloy wheels. The finish on the bodywork (and later on the fully faired Vampire's heavy fairing) were

BIKE FACT   First Built 1983

Lord Hesketh created both a Grand Prix racing team and an aristocratic motorcycle.

exquisite. The 90-degree air-cooled four-stroke
vee-twin was developed by the experts at
Weslake, with four cams, four valves per cylinder
and, in sportiest form, 80bhp from 992cc. It
looked stunning but it never quite delivered. It
needed development, and there was neither time
nor, finally, funds. It would hit 125mph and in
spite of its weight, handled and stopped well, but
it had many detail mechanical problems and both
the bike and the company were, sadly, short-lived.

Honda CB450 Black Bomber

In the beginning, Japan made small, economical four-strokes and screaming, exotic two-strokes. Not big, sporty four-strokes. The complacent British industry saw that as their domain. Then, in 1965, along came the Honda CB450 Black Bomber, nicknamed for its original black paint scheme, although later models also came in red. Suddenly, Japan did make a bigger four-stroke, and a good one – a modern one. The 445cc CB450 was a parallel twin but its pistons moved 180 degrees apart rather than together, giving better balance. It had two overhead camshafts instead of pushrods, an exotic layout more typical of racing than road bikes. It had torsion valve springs and a short stroke, so it revved freely and developed 43bhp, enough to worry many British 500s and 650s. The rest was essentially conventional – single-tube cradle frame,

BIKE FACT   First Built 1965

Named for its all-black paint scheme, the Black Bomber dealt a blow to the British motorcycle industry.

telescopic front, swinging-arm rear, drum brakes and four-speed gearbox. It would touch 105mph and was smooth and comfortable at high speeds. A five-speed gearbox and more power improved flexibility in 1967, but it was never totally reliable, didn't handle well or sell in great numbers. But it was the thin end of the wedge.

Honda CB400-Four

While Honda superbikes were adding capacity, a different direction was making a virtue of the smaller, more compact alternative. There was no better illustration of that than the delightful little CB400-Four, introduced in 1975 and aimed squarely at Europe.

The four-cylinder route to the 400 was from CB750 superbike, downsized to the much-loved CB500, briefly via the underachieving CB350, and back to the hugely better CB400-Four itself. It has often been described as a small superbike and in its way it was. It was beautifully packaged, with sporty looks, no superfluous weight and a distinctive, attractive, four-into-one exhaust system. It had a capacity of 408cc from virtually square bore and stroke dimensions, a single overhead camshaft, two valves per cylinder and four carburettors. It developed 37bhp and its

BIKE FACT   First Built 1975

The 400-Four was a classic on a smaller scale, showing Europe that size isn't everything.

crankshaft configuration made it sound gloriously like a small F1 car engine. It was good for just over 100mph and loved to be revved hard and ridden quickly, making full use of its six-speed gearbox and agile, predictable handling. Even with the 1977 CB400F2 it changed very little, until, ironically, it was overtaken by the CB400T twin, which was far less sophisticated and characterful but both faster and cheaper.

Honda CB750

No question, this was the one that broke the mould and showed the future of bikes. When it was launched, in 1969, the CB750 was lauded by every tester as being in a class of its own and, for once, this opinion was even confirmed by the sales figures. Honda didn't present it as a sports bike, rather as a fast all-rounder, but to most it remains the first modern superbike.

Its heart was the first full production four-cylinder engine in a bike. By modern standards the engine was simple, with only one overhead camshaft and eight valves, but it was free-revving, reliable and bursting with character. It delivered an excellent 67bhp – maybe ten more horsepower than its British rival twins and triples. It was fast, with a top speed of 124mph, it was attractive, with its two pairs of splayed chrome exhausts, and it was sophisticated. It had a five-speed

BIKE FACT   First Built 1969

Regarded as the first Japanese superbike, the CB750 was the writing on the wall for the old school.

gearbox and electric starting. It pioneered the hydraulic front disc brake, it was generally unburstable and temperament-free, and being a four-cylinder it was extremely smooth for quick long-distance cruising. It was no lightweight, and it didn't pretend to be a sports bike in today's sense, but it handled just about well enough to do justice to its mighty performance and it was never better than in its original form.

Honda NSR500

Because Honda's success was based on four-strokes, they stuck with them in 500cc racing for longer than they should have done. But even the complex late-1970s NR500 never won a championship and in 1983 Honda finally made a 500 two-stroke racer. It was the incredible NS500, with which Freddie Spencer took Honda's first 500 title.

That triple won more through handling than power but its successor, the NSR500, soon changed that. It was a liquid-cooled 90-degree vee-four, and where rivals used twin cranks the NSR500 had one, with narrow, low-friction bearings. It had crankcase reed valves, four carburettors and awesome power (allegedly more than 140bhp in 1984), in an unconventional frame with fuel tank below engine and exhausts above. By 1985 the layout had reverted to normal

BIKE FACT   First Built 1983
Honda's first two-stroke racer was technically advanced, unconventional, very powerful and a winner.

and the NSR500 had won its first title, through sheer power and speed rather than through handling. In fact the NSR500 was difficult to ride, but it went on to win further titles in 1987 and 1989 through brute force. It extracted maximum power at the expense of a tiny rev-range until revisions in the early 1990s made it slightly more user-friendly but more powerful still, with more than 185bhp and the first ever race-recorded 200mph maximum.

Honda CBX1000

Benelli and the Sei may have beaten them into six-cylinder production but in 1978 with the CBX1000, Honda (who had already done pretty well with racing sixes) made the road-bike format work properly. It was something of a statement: they did it because they could, not because they had to, Honda already having some of the fastest bikes in the world in their catalogue.

The layout is inevitably difficult – six cylinders in-line across the frame can only be wide and weighty. But Honda didn't compromise and make the CBX a big, soft tourer, they made it a relatively lean and agile sports bike. All things are relative; lean here meant around 575lb, a hefty weight reined in by double front and single rear discs. Handling was surprisingly faithful thanks to well-controlled suspension and a very stiff diamond backbone frame using the big engine as

BIKE FACT   First Built 1978

The CBX wasn't just Honda's first six-cylinder production bike, it was the first six that really worked.

a stressed unit. That air-cooled six was 1047cc, with twin overhead cams, 24 valves, six carburettors and 105bhp. It was canted well forwards to accommodate the carbs and ancillaries and drove through a five-speed gearbox and chain final drive. It gave the CBX1000 a super-smooth top speed of 135mph, and that was enough for most.

Honda CB1100R

The *raison d'être* for the CB1100R was straightforward: it was designed to win production endurance races, specifically in the southern hemisphere markets of South Africa and Australia. It was introduced in 1981 and built in no more than the requisite numbers – 1000 examples – almost regardless of cost. Its natural habitat was the race track, but of necessity it was road-legal, and it also happened to be a superb road bike. It was powered by an enlarged version of the CB900 engine, bored to 1062cc. It was an air-cooled twin-cam 16-valve transversely-mounted in-line four, with four carburettors and driving through a five-speed gearbox and chain final drive. With extensive tuning it gave 115bhp, which made it the world's most powerful production motorcycle, and in a package weighing just less than 520lb it would

BIKE FACT First Built 1981
Race-bred and race-liveried, the CB1100R was successful way beyond the tiny numbers sold.

reach 140mph in road trim. More than that, it was considered to be one of the best-handling big bikes of its generation – probably the best. It had a strengthened version of the 900's twin-downtube frame and air-assisted front forks, adjustable twin-shock rear suspension. It had triple disc brakes and red-and-white liveried fairing – and it was a winner, on road and track.

Honda CBR600F

When the CBR600F was launched in 1987 it didn't break new ground in terms of design or engineering but it did offer a subtly different character from all those superbikes and race replicas. It brought Honda back into a major sector that they had been losing out in for too long – the affordable sports tourer. It had the looks, with its fully enveloping bodywork and bold graphics providing its most novel design element. It had the engineering, with a diamond frame, anti-dive forks, rear monoshock, triple-disc brakes and six-speed gearbox. But by keeping expensive materials and detail frills to a minimum, it managed to be affordable too. The other key cost-cutter was Honda's overdue switch back from vee-four to simpler in-line four engines, and there was nothing wrong with the CBR600F's. It was liquid-cooled, twin-cam, 16-

BIKE FACT   First Built 1987

The CBR600F bucked the trend of the 1980s by being short on expensive details but still big on character.

valve and it was both light and compact, without being unduly exotic. It managed an impressive 85bhp which took the 400lb bike to a genuine 140mph, well matched by very good handling and total lack of temperament. Even with sales already leading the class, Honda continued to improve the CBR600F – first with 93bhp and in 1991 endowing it with 100bhp, which took the top speed to well over 150mph.

Honda NS400

The NS400 was Honda's roadgoing tribute to the NS500 with which Freddie Spencer won their first 500 championship in 1983. Given the exotic specification of the two-stroke racer you realise why the words are 'tribute to' and not 'replica of'. The engine was a liquid-cooled 90-degree vee-three, in the NS400's case with a capacity of 387cc. It used reed valves and an ATAC exhaust power valve to improve low-range torque and give a reasonable rev band so long as you used the close-ratio six-speed gearbox. The chassis was a box-section alloy frame with anti-dive front suspension, clothed in a fairing which was a close replica of the 500 racer, in red, white and blue. The engine was turned around from the racing layout to have the single cylinder vertical and the outer pair horizontal and pointing forwards, with carburettors in the vee for a compact package in

BIKE FACT   First Built 1983

In 1983 Freddie Spencer gave Honda its first 500 title; in tribute, Honda gave us the evocative NS400.

both length and width. It was very light, very powerful with 72bhp and very quick, with a maximum of more than 130mph and shattering mid-range acceleration once into its power band. It also had handling and brakes good enough to do justice to the image.

Honda CBR1000F

Launched alongside the CBR600F in 1987, the CBR1000F was another new-generation water-cooled in-line four-stroke four from Honda. It was also another bike capitalising on a huge market for sporting machines at reasonable cost, without going to the outer fringes of expensive technology – using a steel perimeter frame, for example, rather than aluminium alloy. It was Honda's answer to the Kawasaki GPz1000 and it won the battle, in both performance and sales. This bigger of the two new Honda four sports roadsters originally developed 133bhp from its short-stroke 16-valve four-carburettor engine and, although it was no lightweight at nearly 500lb dry, that gave it a top speed of 162mph. With gear-driven balancer shaft it was if anything even smoother than the smaller new four, and the whole bike was perfect for its market niche –

BIKE FACT　　　　　First Built 1987
The fast but affordable CBR1000F showed that Honda could still recognise an under-served market niche.

stylish, fast, comfortable and with more than adequate handling, like the engineering stopping just short of the outer sports-bike limits. One of its best features was its excellent flexibility, pulling hard from low down before getting even stronger in the middle and turning into a real screamer at the top, but there was a great deal else to recommend it.

Honda VFR750/RC30

The VFR750R, also known as the RC30, was Honda's homologation route to World Superbike racing eligibility in the late 1980s – and a championship winner from the start. It was widely used as an off-the-shelf customer racing model, but as the rules demanded it was road-legal, and possibly the most extreme street bike Honda had ever built when it was launched in 1988. It was directly descended from the super-successful RVF750 works endurance racer and was hand built and totally uncompromising. It was powered by a liquid-cooled, double overhead camshaft, 16-valve, 90-degree, four-stroke vee-four of 748cc, developing a smooth, quite flexible and gloriously musical 112bhp, delivered through a six-speed gearbox with a high first gear and racing-close ratios. It used a massive but feather-light twin-beam aluminium box frame,

BIKE FACT   First Built 1988

Road-legal but to all intents race-ready, the RC30 was a direct descendant of the RVF750 endurance racer.

air-assisted front forks, single-sided swinging arm and monoshock rear suspension. With its short wheelbase, near perfect balance and riding position, and race-developed handling and brakes, it was widely regarded as the greatest of all the racer clones. In 'normal' production form it was good for over 156mph, and there were factory options to give 130bhp and even more speed.

Honda CBR900RR FireBlade

In 1992 Honda's CBR900RR FireBlade rewrote the sports bike rule book as Honda introduced what at least one very experienced tester called '1000cc power in a 600cc-sized package'. And that put Honda firmly back on top of the ultimate four-cylinder sports bike pile, for at least six years. Its big advantage was an exceptionally low weight, almost exactly 400lb, which meant that the quoted tester was not exaggerating with his 600cc comparison.

The FireBlade's twin-beam frame was all aluminium alloy with an extremely short wheelbase and virtually upright front forks, a combination that gave lightning-quick responses. Into the frame went a water-cooled in-line four-cylinder four-stroke engine with twin cams, 16 valves and a silky-smooth, eager-to-rev character. In its original 893cc form the FireBlade

BIKE FACT   First Built 1992

Power handling and dramatic looks came together to make the FireBlade *the* 1990s superbike.

had produced a gruff 122bhp, but later with 919cc that was to go up to a more softly delivered 128bhp. In either case such power was enough to give the lightweight 'Blade sensational performance, including a quoted top speed of 167mph as well as sub-11-second standing quarter-mile times which left any other 1992 bike for dead. Yet quite apart from that, the CBR900RR had the most usable performance of any bike then on the road, with superbly controlled suspension and, again, all the advantages of a bike of such a light weight.

Honda CBR1100XX Blackbird

Get ready for the big numbers. In 1997 Honda went back to the tops of both the maximum power and maximum speed lists with the CBR1100XX Blackbird, which mustered 164bhp in a bike weighing less than 500lb, and a maximum of as much as 186mph – figures unrivalled until the arrival of the mighty Suzuki Hayabusa. It was performance through science and with finesse. The power came from an 1137cc twin-cam 16-valve in-line four-cylinder engine, originally with carburettors, later with injection for a smoother power curve. But another part of the secret was that the Blackbird also has low weight and superb aerodynamics, with small frontal area and very slippery shape, which for all its massive performance potential makes it both lightly stressed and a comfortable, docile, relaxing high-speed cruiser. Not to mention a genuine

BIKE FACT   First Built 1997

By the late 1990s the limits for big superbikes had moved way out, but none further than the Blackbird.

two-seater. So no, it isn't a race-clone, it's more an ultra-quick super-versatile sophisticate. Its longish wheelbase and well raked forks work slightly against the fastest reactions, and amazing though it sounds, the Blackbird is perfectly happy as a touring bike, mechanically refined, with terrific linked brakes, comfortable in both ride and wind protection, and as superbly built as any Honda.

Indian 101 Scout

The Indian company, at one time the world's biggest motorcycle manufacturer, made many fine motorcycles, but possibly none better than the Model 101 Scout, introduced in 1928. Like rival Harley-Davidson, Indian made a virtue of the big, slow-revving, stump-pulling vee-twin, in their case usually with a cylinder angle of 42 degrees rather than the Harley's 45, which made for a subtly different character. For Indian, Chiefs were the big bikes and Scouts, which first appeared in 1920, the middleweights. The 101 had a 750cc – or 45cu in – sidevalve engine, originally developing some 18bhp, which was enough for a top speed of around 75mph in showroom tune or 100mph with Indian's racing options. The biggest advance for the 101 over earlier Scouts, though, was a sporty new frame, which had a familiar layout of twin cradle tubes and quarter-elliptic

BIKE FACT   First Built 1928

Indians were eventually overshadowed by Harleys, but they once had a bigger company.

leaf-sprung leading-link front forks, but now
gained front brakes for the first time and was
longer and lower than before, which made it
more comfortable, better-handling and easier to
stop. The Scout also had a reputation for
reliability and it was undeniably stylish, but
within a couple of years it grew heavier and
much less special.

Indian 648 Scout

The Sport Scout, the model that replaced the 101 Scout in 1934 as a rival to the Harley 45s, became a long-running line for Indian, and a very racy one. The first were 45cu in (745cc), with girder-fork frame, streamlined mudguards and a new Indian-head badge on the teardrop tank. Offering performance with style, they were frequently the light and compact basis for production racing efforts, and the Daytona engine option was named for the Scout's win in the Daytona 200 in 1937. After a successful life, with steady mechanical and styling development, and having been the basis for many Indian military machines in the 1940s, the last of the Sports Scouts appeared in 1948, and it was the sportiest of them all. Developed from the bike that won the 1947 Daytona 200, it was dubbed the 648 Daytona Scout, and had an improved version of

BIKE FACT   First Built 1948

The tragedy of the Scout was that it was one of Indian's sportiest bikes but also one of its last.

the 45-degree 45cu in sidevalve vee-twin, whose
enlarged sump gave it the nickname 'big base', in
a frame with an eye to racing. With a top speed of
over 100mph, it did the job, with another
Daytona win in 1948, but against a background of
financial troubles, just fifty were built.

Kawasaki 500 Mach III

Having failed to achieve much sales or critical success in the mid-1960s with its early big bikes (including an unashamedly English 650 parallel-twin four-stroke, the W1), Kawasaki returned to a different, two-stroke tack, and a new lease of life. In 1969, after some modest success with smallish two-stroke twins, they hit the jackpot with the very exciting 500cc H1, or Mach III. It was exciting in more ways than one.

It was a good-looking, compact, light and powerful air-cooled, in-line, transverse triple. It produced 60bhp, which gave it an incredible power-to-weight ratio, but it would be fair to say that its delivery was rather sudden, starting gently but with big power arriving in a huge, nerve-testing rush towards the top of the rev range. Add to that high-speed Mr Hyde act a twin-tube frame with a reputation for being flexible and

BIKE FACT   First Built 1969

The Mach III was a two-stoke wonder: light, fast and almost too exciting.

unpredictable and you had a spectacular handling package. What was undeniable was that it was very quick in a straight line (if you could keep it in one), with a top speed of around 120mph which would eat many bigger bikes in its day; but most called it character-building.

Kawasaki 750 H2

Going from H1 to H2 and Mach III to Mach IV, Kawasaki's two-stroke triple gained more capacity, a good deal more power, a marginally more user-friendly handling package and an even wilder reputation.

Enlarged to 748cc and with the same throttle-sensitive venom that made the H1 infamous, the screaming short-stroke three-pot produced 74bhp in 1970. It promised 125mph, and 12.5-second standing quarters. Even 'marginally better' is a generous description of the H2's hair-trigger handling. Weight distribution was still too rear-biased, so while it helped traction it also encouraged both wheelies and lack of steering effectiveness. Similarly, the frame was still way too lightly engineered and worryingly flexible (even towards the end of its life, when it was mildly strengthened, the

---

BIKE FACT   First Built 1970

The H2 became a legend, both for its speed and for its wayward personality.

geometry tweaked and the power slightly softened). There were other drawbacks. The bike was far from comfortable, the engine far from smooth, and it was both thirsty and smoky. The 750 H2 became a legend as much because of its frightening manners as in spite of them. It was frequently a white-knuckle ride, but there was no denying it was quick, so long as the rider was its equal. Few were, and in the end emissions regulations intervened.

Kawasaki Z1

After Honda's CB750 created the modern superbike genre in 1969, Kawasaki responded in 1972 with the Z1, a four-stroke four which was as well-rounded and mature as Kawasaki's two-stroke triples were delinquent. It had a capacity of 903cc, and where the Honda had a single overhead camshaft the Kawasaki had two. The shafts were gear-driven where the Honda's was chain-driven, and they operated two valves per cylinder. It produced 82bhp, which up until then had been strictly top-end race-bike territory. In barely 500lb of bike that meant it offered 133mph – which was enough, finally, to knock the CB750 off its perch. It looked wonderful, and it was smooth, competitively priced and reliable as well as fast. Like the Kawasaki strokers, its frame wasn't its best feature, but at least the Z1's handling stopped short of being laughable. It had

BIKE FACT   First Built 1972

Speed and great looks ensured that the Z1 became a classic bike.

a twin-tube cradle, rather meanly-sized front
telescopic forks and in the beginning one front
disc and a rear drum. Like the two-strokes it
wasn't entirely user-friendly, but it had acceptable
balance between comfort and predictability, so
long as you didn't abuse it. It was steadily
developed, with twin front discs from 1976, on
what then became the Z900 – final step to the
Z1000 in 1977.

Kawasaki Z1300

Towards the end of the 1970s, with its once-dominant 900s and 1000s leapfrogged (or at least chased) by increasingly powerful challengers from Japanese rivals, Kawasaki adopted the age-old principle that there's no substitute for cubic inches, and in 1979 launched the Z1300. It went the six-cylinder route, and did it superbly. It had a different character from most of its rivals, and especially different from recent Kawasakis. It was immensely powerful and quick, but this time as a long-legged and unburstable tourer rather than as a frenetic point-and-squirt sports bike. The liquid-cooled straight-six had a capacity of

BIKE FACT   First Built 1979

The combination of six cylinders and shaft drive meant effortless speed in the Z1300.

1286cc, two overhead camshafts, two valves per cylinder and initially three twin-choke carburettors. Later electronic fuel injection made it even smoother, more powerful and more economical. From the start it delivered 120bhp, later 130bhp, which gave top speeds rising from around 135mph to more than 140mph. It had the smooth luxury of shaft-drive, behind a five-speed gearbox. For a sports bike it was simply too big and heavy and its styling too conservative, but as an effortlessly fast and comfortable all-rounder it was in a class of its own.

Kawasaki Z1-RTC Turbo

One thing about Kawasaki in the 1970s, you could hardly accuse them of not pushing the envelope. Never mind the scary two-strokes and the big-hitting four-stroke fours and sixes, how about a Z1R with turbocharging?

It was a factory-assisted project as opposed to a pure works bike, and a limited edition, conceived by a former vice president of Kawasaki of North America, and ultimately made in a run of around 1600 examples.

You have to acknowledge the RTC Turbo for its sheer bravado. The starting point was the air-cooled four-cylinder twin-cam Z1R engine, onto which were grafted a compact turbocharger and a single large carburettor, cleverly tucked in behind the cylinders with some very snaky exhaust plumbing. It stopped quite well with the Z1R's triple discs, and it needed to. With around

---

BIKE FACT   First Built 1978

While not a factory bike, this RTC Turbo was a useful turbo testbed for Kawasaki.

125bhp in a standard Z1R frame that had only recently been persuaded to handle properly with 90bhp, it was a bit of a beast. Not surprisingly it was phenomenal in a straight line, capable of running sub-11-second quarter-mile times and going on to maxima that nobody has quoted, perhaps because nobody has been brave enough to measure them. But it has to be said it wasn't particularly keen on corners.

Kawasaki Z750 Turbo

Having put a toe in the water of turbocharging in 1978 with the limited-edition, officially unofficial Z1-RTC Turbo, Kawasaki went one better in 1983 and produced a real production turbocharged road bike – ironically making them the last of the Japanese big four to do so. But theirs was the one that really worked.

Based on the unblown Z750 and with a capacity of 738cc, it was bigger than any of its rivals and more blatantly aimed at outright performance. The air-cooled twin-cam in-line four with blower made 112bhp, and in a motorbike weighing little more than the ordinary 750 that delivered almost 150mph. But it wasn't only peak power and the very high top speed that made the Kawasaki Turbo installation so impressive, it was its overall delivery. Earlier turbo bikes with long exhaust tracts had suffered

BIKE FACT   First Built 1983
The Z750 Turbo had mountains of performance, but unlike its contemporaries, it was user-friendly.

the nightmare of turbo-lag. The Kawasaki somehow managed to squeeze the tiny turbo in front of the cylinders, virtually onto the exhaust ports, so it had negligible lag and, further helped by Kawasaki's excellent electronically managed injection system, had a remarkably smooth power curve, without any huge rush of additional boost. And its performance went on to be rewarded with sales success, as it both outsold and outlasted its rivals.

Kawasaki GPz900R

The GPz900R, launched in 1984, was a hi-tech
showcase for Kawasaki, which used new design
and manufacturing techniques to answer the old
problem of a water-cooled transverse in-line four-
cylinder engine being wider than was really
desirable. Rather than a conventional full water
jacket around the cylinder block, the GPz900R
pioneered what were called 'wet liners' around
the individual cylinders, helping make the engine
several inches narrower than a conventional
engine of similar capacity. It also had double
overhead camshafts and four valves per cylinder,
contributing to an output of 119bhp in a
wonderfully compact package, clothed in almost
full bodywork that was also more modern than
the early 1980s norm. That all added up to a top
speed of almost 160mph and handling that was
faithful rather than fantastic, but maybe the best

BIKE FACT   First Built 1984
In order to get bigger, 'big-capacity' bike engines had to
get smaller; with the GPz900R, Kawasaki showed how.

thing of all about the GPz900R was that it developed into the GPz1000R, which Kawasaki in 1985 thought was the fastest bike they would ever allow themselves to build. With capacity up to 997cc and power to 125bhp, that finally broke the 160mph barrier. However, once the world had got used to the idea of 160mph, it was just another step on the ladder.

Kawasaki ZX-10

In 1988, having clearly rethought their voluntary moratorium on increasing top speeds, Kawasaki introduced the ZX-10. It was a machine capable of 168mph and it would take them screaming into the 1990s as continuing holders of the 'world's fastest' title.

It was a take-no-prisoners step up from the GPz1000R, a liquid-cooled twin-cam 16-valve in-line 997cc four that developed a truly remarkable 135bhp. The engine was also wonderfully flexible, showing a tractable nature once it was out of the lower reaches and into its mighty stride. Its full fairing advertised its 'E-Box frame', an aluminium alloy perimeter in which the E stood for Egg, and referred to the oval shape of the big side members. It had a six-speed gearbox, chain final drive and very fine twin-front, single-rear disc brakes. It also had a 17-

---

BIKE FACT   First Built 1988

Big, comfortable and not overly sporty, the ZX-10 was another 'world's fastest bike' from Kawasaki.

inch front wheel and 18-inch rear, reflecting the amount of power it had to put down. It wasn't aggressively sporty, it was actually quite soft and comfortable, as befitted its size and weight, but even with the drag of a big fairing and a riding position that would take you a long way without your body setting rigid, it was still the fastest bike on the block, until the next Kawasaki.

Kawasaki ZXR750

World Superbike racing isn't only a showplace for manufacturers, it's a marketplace for customer racing models, into which Kawasaki's 1989 newcomer was the ZXR750. And, of course, the starting point onto which the off-the-shelf racers can graft track-specific performance is also a fully road-legal sports bike – and more so in the case of the very affordable, not over-exotic ZXR750 than most Superbike rivals can claim. It has a relatively simple chassis with bold, racer bodywork and graphics. The frame is an aluminium alloy twin beam, suspension is fully adjustable and even for the road it is noticeably firm. The engine is derived from the more mundane GPX750 road

BIKE FACT   First Built 1989

For some, the ZXR750 was the start of the path to World Superbike racing; to others, it was a road bike.

bike, a liquid-cooled, twin-cam in-line four of
748cc, only mildly tuned for the basic version of
the ZXR750, to give 108bhp, but with plenty
more bolt-on horsepower readily available for the
real racers – and regular updates for all. In road
trim the ZXR750 pulled just over 150mph, and
because its chassis is designed to cope with
considerably more its handling and stopping are
impeccable, although ride comfort is virtually
zero. It was a championship winner by 1993, and
commercially a winner from the start.

Kawasaki ZZ-R1100

In 1990 Kawasaki continued its claim to the world's fastest production bike title with the ZZ-R1100, and the ZZ-R1100 hung onto its position for much of the decade, until the coming of the Honda CBR1100XX Blackbird and the Suzuki GSX1300R Hayabusa. Its 1052cc engine was developed from the ZX-10's, a liquid-cooled, twin-cam, 16-valve four with bigger bores and very short stroke. It used 'ram' air-intake technology similar to that seen in modern Formula One cars, to force air into the carburettors, picking it up via a forward-facing duct below the headlamp and feeding it back to a sealed air-box. That also helped keep the intake air cooler, and therefore denser, than normal. In some markets power was voluntarily restricted to 125bhp by carburettor restrictors, for others it was an unrestricted and ferocious 145bhp, giving

---

BIKE FACT   First Built 1990

Using Formula One car technology, the ZZ-R1100 held the fastest bike title until Honda's Blackbird in 1997.

the ZZ-R1100 a top speed of 175mph, acceleration to match, and the undisputed fastest title. Equally important, the ZZ-R1100 was very road-friendly, more super-quick tourer than race clone, with six-speed gearbox, comfortable room for two and fine handling based on a super-strong aluminium perimeter frame and very stiff box-section swing-arm.

Laverda 750SFC

Having come into the motorcycle market in 1949, from the manufacture of agricultural machinery via small commuter bikes and scooters, in the late 1960s Laverda finally discovered performance, and ever since has been known for it. 1968 was the year when they produced their first big twin, initially a superbly engineered Honda-lookalike 650 parallel-twin four-stroke, which was quickly uprated to 744cc and marketed in two forms, as the 750GT tourer and the 750S sports bike. They were successful, and they were excellent bikes, not only quick but with strong backbone frames, light weight and race-ready handling, which made them regular endurance race winners in the late 1960s and early 1970s. Reflecting that, Laverda launched an even sportier version of the 750, the 750SF, which developed a smooth and willing 65bhp and gave a top speed of around 118mph,

BIKE FACT   First Built 1971

It took Laverda a while to move from tiny runabouts to big sports bikes but their early 750s made the leap.

on a beautifully lithe and uncluttered-looking machine, if not a particularly comfortable one for roadgoing purposes. At the top of the 750 range was the rare and expensive 750SFC, the lightest and most powerful of the bunch, with racing-style half fairing, 70bhp, initially with big drum brakes but later twin front discs, and a top speed of around 130mph.

Laverda Montjuic 500

Laverda may have been best known in the 1970s for its big triples, and especially the Jota, but alongside them the Italian company made some very fine smaller bikes, including its excellent 500 twins. The mainstream model was the 500 Alpina, which was yet another Italian variation on the 500 theme, alongside Guzzi's shaft-driven vee-twin, Ducati's desmo café racer and Benelli's Honda-cloned four. The Laverda was a twin-overhead camshaft eight-valve parallel twin, its angular and close-finned finning making it look just like a baby Jota with one cylinder lopped off. It sat in a single-tube frame with conventional but nicely tuned telescopic front

BIKE FACT   First Built 1978

Laverda created the 'Formula 500' model as a 'one-make' race series special to promote the 500 in Italy.

and swinging-arm rear suspension, and triple disc brakes, with cast-iron discs. It had a capacity of 497cc and twin carburettors, and in the sportiest version, the Montjuic, it had a bit more than the basic Alpina's 44bhp – but Laverda didn't say how much. It drove through a slick-shifting six-speed gearbox, and the Montjuic had sporty touches like a small nose fairing, rear-set aluminium footrests, and fairly rudimentary silencers on a revised exhaust system. It was very noisy, reasonably smooth for a twin, and capable of around 115mph.

Laverda Jota

Having established their performance credentials with the sporting 750 twins, Laverda underlined them, in bold, with a magnificent family of triples, which started with the 3C in 1973. That had a typically handsome and well-finished Laverda four-stroke engine with the characteristic close-pitched cooling fins. An in-line, transverse triple, it had a capacity of 981cc and twin overhead camshafts to give 80bhp, in a bike that was both substantially engineered and aggressively styled. More successful and more famous was its offspring the Jota, originally devised by Laverda's British importers and introduced in 1976. The 3C engine was uprated with higher compression, bigger carbs and special camshafts and exhausts – to give 90bhp and a top speed of around 140mph. It became a frequent production bike race winner and one of the most distinctive road bikes ever,

BIKE FACT   First Built 1976

The Jota was a Laverda icon: totally uncompromising, brimming with character, flawed but unforgettable.

with its characteristic 180-degree three-cylinder engine note (later softened, sadly, with a more conventional 120-degree crank) and the astounding mid-range flexibility that that layout endowed. In a solid, if not outstanding, twin cradle frame, with conventional 1970s suspension, five-spoke alloy wheels and outstanding triple disc brakes, it was a package as muscular and uncompromising as it looked.

Laverda RGS Corsa

While the first-generation Laverda triples had outstanding power, they had some serious compromises. The 180-degree crankshaft layout, which had the outer pistons at the tops of their strokes while the middle piston was at the bottom, gave exceptional low-speed flexibility and that sensationally hard-edged engine noise, but it also gave nightmare vibrations which made bikes like the 3C and Jota anything but relaxing. The next generation addressed that with a total redesign, adopting a 120-degree crankshaft which evened out the firing pulses, the vibration (further softened by new rubber engine mounts) and (the main bad news) the unique

BIKE FACT First Built 1983

Softer and more civilised than the Jota, perhaps, but the next-generation Laverda triples added refinement.

exhaust note. This revised engine, in 981cc form
with 95bhp, was the heart of the RGS Corsa,
sportiest of the new triples, launched in 1983.
Similarly quick at 140mph, it was rather more
civilised than its predecessor the Jota, and more
softly styled with its slippery part-fairing and tall
screen. It was more refined, clearly, and perhaps
more rider-friendly, but it didn't have quite so
much character and it was no longer faster than
its Japanese contemporaries, while company
financial problems and more stringent emissions
requirements were also closing in on it.

Moto Guzzi 850 Le Mans

Amazingly, the distinctive transverse vee-twin engine characteristic of all the sportiest Moto Guzzis started life in the early 1960s as a workhorse engine for a strange little military three-wheeler and later a Guzzi military motorcycle. The engine's strength was its fantastic torque, which guaranteed its adoption for future Guzzi road bikes, forever more.

The first appeared in 1967, as the V7, with 703cc and 40bhp. In 1969 that grew into the 757cc, 45bhp V7 Special, and in 1972 the much less frumpy V7 Sport, with more power and a more compact and nimble frame. The most famous of the sporting Guzzis appeared with the 850 Le Mans, in 1976. The basics remained the same as before, the 90-degree vee-twin with its pushrod overhead valves still sitting transversely across the twin-tube frame and keeping shaft

BIKE FACT   First Built 1976

The vee-twin Guzzis could never be accused of being technically exotic, but they have always been special.

drive. But the whole bike was both lower and lighter than its predecessors, and with a neat nose fairing, sexy exhausts, very low seat and clip-on-type bars, it looked wonderful. The twin-front, single-rear disc brakes were interconnected for excellent balance and the 844cc engine was tuned to give 71bhp and a maximum of around 130mph, but it was the bike's wonderful handling as much as its performance that made the Le Mans so outstanding.

MV Agusta 750S

Motorcycle names don't come much more illustrious than MV Agusta and 1970s sports bikes didn't come much more exotic or exclusive than the 1970 MV Agusta 750 Sport and its descendants. MV had an immaculate racing pedigree, and its road bikes had performance, style and image by the bucketful. Remarkably, the 750 Sport was MV's first genuinely sporty four-cylinder road bike, after some rather underachieving tourers, but it was worth waiting for. It was a pure thoroughbred, from its immaculate engine castings to its screaming high-speed exhaust note, its pared-down racer looks and its evocative red-white-and-blue livery. Its air-cooled transverse four-cylinder engine looked like no other with its tightly-finned barrels, widely splayed twin cam covers over the gear-driven camshafts, ram-piped carburettors and four

BIKE FACT   First Built 1970

In motorcycle terms, MV is Italian for thoroughbred, but it was a while before these bikes took the sporty route.

individual, paired megaphone exhausts. Its huge front drum brake had racing-style cooling duct and strut base. Everything about the 750 Sport (except perhaps the fact that it used shaft drive) screamed performance, and it delivered. The 743cc engine produced 69bhp, and although the Agusta was no lightweight it hit 120mph, accompanied by the most exquisite, race-bred soundtrack and the expensive waft of exclusivity.

MV Agusta 850 Monza

In 1977 MV Agusta emerged from a period in the fast-bike doldrums with another classic sports roadster that at the time looked to be a swansong for the financially troubled motorcycle arm of the company, which had increasingly become an expensive and indulgent sideline to the main business of building helicopters. The bike was the 850 Monza, a further development of the 750S America, which in its turn was an American market development of the brilliant 750 Sport. The America had taken capacity to 789cc, power to 75bhp and top speed to around 130mph. The Monza raised the stakes again, to 837cc, probably some 90bhp (though MV didn't quote figures) and a top speed of over 145mph, which put them right back into the superbike end of the market. But it wasn't only the performance that was super about the Monza. It had all MV's familiar image

BIKE FACT   First Built 1977

Building helicopters was Agusta's mainstay, but building sporting bikes was what made it famous.

of power and style, with its four big exhausts and the characteristic dull finish of its sand-cast engine and gearbox casings. And of course, it had the MV magic in its super-taut handling, its powerful triple cast-iron disc brakes, the distinctive mechanical howl and the sheer exclusivity – if only for a couple of years.

MV Agusta 750F4

Under the new ownership of Cagiva, MV Agusta escaped extinction and in 1999 unveiled their most sensational road bike ever, variously described by testers as the world's most formidable multi-cylinder motorcycle, and the superbike for the millennium. The F4 was designed and built without compromise – like the two-wheeled equivalent of the McLaren F1 supercar, an ultimate statement. Its aggressive lines and visible mechanical details, not least the four exhausts below the seat, are exquisite. Its specification is on the outer limits. The engine is a super-compact liquid-cooled in-line 750 four, with four radial valves per cylinder, downdraught

---

BIKE FACT   First Built 1999

Another famous Italian marque had a hand in the F4, Ferrari contributed to its engine design.

injection intakes, and 130bhp at a screaming 12,500rpm. It delivers 170mph, with huge flexibility matched by a six-speed cassette gearbox, while the F4's frame technology, light weight, perfect balance and super compact dimensions give it breathtaking steering and handling. The engine is a stressed element, in a trellis of steel tubes and magnesium castings carrying state-of-the-art front telescopics and rear monoshock. With two six-pot front disc brakes to do most of the stopping and a new generation of Pirelli tyres providing the grip, the F4 is destined to be an all-time great.

Münch Mammoth 4 1200TTS

More than a few people have tried to squeeze car engines into one-off special bikes; German dealer turned bike builder Friedl Münch put them into production. His first specially-commissioned project in 1966 used an air-cooled four-cylinder single-overhead cam NSU Prinz 1000 car engine, with bespoke clutch and modified four-speed Horex gearbox in a hand-made steel tube duplex cradle frame with bulbous aluminium tank, enclosed chain drive and huge magnesium front drum brake. It easily achieved its target of 200kph, and impressed its first tester enough for Münch to start limited production – with orders coming in far quicker than expected, in spite of a price to match the bike's size and weight. The ungainly-looking machine was extensively modified to improve reliability and give acceptable handling (although that wasn't as

BIKE FACT   First Built 1966

The strange-looking Münch Mammoth was one of the widest bikes ever to reach serious production.

important as high-speed cruising comfort) and was launched as the Mammoth. The best-known and most successful of the long-running series was the 1200TTS of the early 1970s, powered by an 1177cc version of the NSU four, giving around 90bhp and a top speed of 125mph or more, in probably the largest and strangest bike ever to reach full production.

Norton International 500

Created in the early 1930s and surviving into the late 1950s, the many versions of the Norton International were early equivalents of today's race replicas – roadgoing versions of the legendary Manx Norton racers, distinguished mainly by the amount of equipment they carried rather than by mechanical specification. The International was launched in 1932; the stripped-down version – named for giving Norton so many successes in the Isle of Man – was the Manx. Both had Norton's recently introduced vertical single-cylinder 497cc engine, using a shaft and bevel-gear-driven single overhead camshaft, operating large valves with exposed springs. From the start the International was a 100mph machine, with the handling, looks and reliability (given dedicated maintenance) to match its speed. After the interruption of World War II, both lines re-

BIKE FACT   First Built 1932

Norton built the International, a roadgoing TT clone, long before the Japanese began building race replicas.

emerged with their familiar road bike, race bike relationship, and better than ever. By 1948 the International had telescopic forks, and in the early 1950s again followed the Manx with the introduction of the famous Featherbed frame, along with improvements to brakes, gearbox and engine. While still popular as the basis for customer race machines, however, it was gradually overshadowed by Norton's new, simpler road bikes, and went out of production in 1958.

Norton Dominator

The Dominator was the road bike that helped push the Norton International off its perch as the 1950s went on. Prompted by the success of Triumph's Speed Twins, the Dominator, unveiled in 1948, used a new parallel vertical twin, pushrod engine, with slightly longer stroke than bore, a capacity of 497cc and a reputation for endlessly willing high-speed cruising, with simpler maintenance than the overhead-cam singles. Originally with plunger rear suspension, from 1953 it had swinging arms, and then the superb Featherbed frame launched in the racing Manx. With 29bhp and a bit more weight it wasn't quite as quick as the International, but a totally reliable top speed of around 90mph and (from 1952, in the Dominator 88) the impeccable handling of the Featherbed frame and strong drum brakes made it an excellent sporting bike

BIKE FACT   First Built 1948
At launch The Dominator was Norton's vertical twin challenger and had decades of development to come.

for a very attractive price. It remained popular, in increasingly well-developed, sporty versions, for many years. By 1956 the Dominator 99 offered 100mph performance, and for many years, including models like the 36bhp 1961 sports special, the frame could have handled much more – some of which Norton provided with the bigger, more powerful Dominator 650SS of 1962, with 49bhp and 110mph-plus.

Norton Commando 850

By the late 1960s Norton's commercial position
was becoming edgy, but the launch of the
Commando in 1968 showed they hadn't yet run
out of interesting bikes. It stuck with the old
British formula of big capacity, long-stroke
parallel twin and robust four-speed gearbox in a
well-developed but otherwise conventional
duplex cradle frame. Conventional, that is, save
for its use of 'Isolastic' rubber mounts to absorb
the inevitable engine vibrations. In its first
incarnation it added a touch of style with its
distinctive 'Fastback' rear fairing. That first
Commando had 745cc and 58bhp for a top speed
of around 115mph. It was quite light, at less than
420lb, and had Norton's traditional fine handling
and grip, with beefy front forks and well-
controlled rear swinging arm. From the start the
Commando had a front disc brake, later models

BIKE FACT   First Built 1968

The Commando's Fastback styling and vibration-
absorbing mounts dragged British bikes into a new era.

had discs front and rear, but in other ways later versions lost some of their edge. In 1974 bigger bores took capacity to 828cc for the Commando 850, but with milder tune for lower emissions, power stayed the same, while American-market expectations like electric start added weight and softened performance, including a maximum down to 110mph, although handling was still excellent.

Norton F1

While struggling to survive, Norton didn't
forsake racing, and even into the early 1970s
could produce a Formula 750 TT winner, using a
light and stiff steel monocoque frame. In theory,
the Norton company had died and gone into
liquidation. But in practice it re-emerged in the
early 1980s, with a long-winded development of
the rotary-engined concept that had first been
mooted a decade before. A 588cc twin-chamber
rotary-engined model was tested by the police,
before a production rotary, the 84bhp
Commander, was launched in 1987. In 1988 and
1989, with sponsorship from John Player, a twin-
spar aluminium-framed Norton rotary racer won
the British F1 championship. And although
sceptics questioned the effective capacity of any
rotary engine, the halo effect was strong enough
to prompt a hand built, limited-edition race-

BIKE FACT   First Built 1989

Norton came back from extinction with the F1, with its
rotary power and innovative frame.

replica sports roadster for 1989, which Norton labelled the F1. It evoked the looks and livery of the 1989 title winner and with exceptional smoothness and pulling power right across the rev range, and an excellent peak output of 94bhp, it was capable of around 150mph, with race-bred brakes, and superb handling from fully adjustable inverted fork front and rising-rate monoshock rear suspension all attached to the racer's aluminium frame.

Rickman Kawasaki CRE

Through the history of motorcycling there have been those who have married up the best of engines and gearboxes from different makes and models, creating Tritons and Tribsas and whatever. And alongside them have been the specialists who built bespoke frames for the best off-the-shelf power, among the best of the latter undoubtedly being the Rickman brothers, Derek and Don.

They learned their craft with motorcross bikes in the late 1960s before building their first production model, the Interceptor, in 1970. That used a 736cc Royal Enfield twin in a superlight, super-stiff steel-tube duplex frame, invariably nickel-plated and carrying excellent suspension and front and rear disc brakes. The frame could clearly be developed to handle more than the Enfield's 56bhp, and soon was, in 1974 for the

---

BIKE FACT　　　　　First Built 1974

One thing the British motorcycle industry could do very well was build superb frames, like the Rickman's.

Honda CB750 four and then for the even more
potent Kawasaki Z1000 four, creating a bike with
the handling and roadholding to match the
Japanese horsepower. The strong and torquey
1015cc twin-cam engine gave 93bhp and with a
standard five-speed Kawasaki gearbox over
130mph, in two versions, the CR and an
'Endurance' model, the CRE, with full, twin-
headlamp endurance-racing type front fairing
and 'fastback' tail.

Rudge Ulster

Rudge was one of the earliest British motorcycle makers and one of its most famous innovators, especially for the Multi, whose ingenious multi-ratio belt-drive system made Rudge a prolific race winner, even a TT winner. In the 1920s the major innovation was a four-valve cylinder head for the 350 and 499cc pushrod-overhead-valve single-cylinder engines, now paired with a conventional four-speed gearbox. An immediate commercial success, it became a famous race winner in the 1928 Ulster Grand Prix, and in honour of the win (repeated in 1929) the 500cc sports machines were dubbed Rudge Ulster, with some 30bhp and a maximum speed of 100mph in sportiest form. Silenced exhausts and lighting kits apart, the extremely light roadgoing Ulsters had the lean look of the racer, and more Rudge innovations, including an effective linked braking system with

BIKE FACT　　　　　First Built 1929
Rudge's Ulster Grand Prix wins in 1928 and 1929 marked the beginning of a long tradition of innovation.

the handlebar lever operating the front drum and the foot pedal both front and rear drums. While racing successes continued with a 1930 Senior TT win (and a Junior win in 1931 for the 250 Rudge), the Depression brought financial problems and although the company (and the Ulster) clung on until 1939, after the war they were no more.

Scott Sprint Special

From his first production model in 1908, there was little about Alfred Scott's motorcycles that was conventional or ordinary. He invented the kickstart, patented caliper-type brakes for bicycles in the 1890s and triangulated frames in 1908, experimented with foot-change gears and telescopic forks and most famously designed highly effective water-cooled parallel-twin two-stroke engines which remained an element of Scott motorcycles through to the firm's demise in the 1950s. The most famous models were the Squirrels, introduced in 1922 and growing into a whole range, including the basic Squirrel, the Flying Squirrel tourer, the Flying Squirrel De Luxe, the Sports Squirrel and the Super Squirrel, variously, by 1930, in capacities from a single-cylinder 298cc to the largest 596cc twin. The 1930 range also included the Power Plus TT

BIKE FACT   First Built 1922

Alfred Scott was a prolific inventor; his motorcycles were never conventional, and often brilliant.

Replica, for road or racing use, the lightweight 245lb Speedway Special adapted specifically for dirt track racing, and rarest of the rare, the Sprint Special, with tuned Power Plus engine, 'for the elect of speedmen', and especially for grasstrack and hillclimb competition. Even the lesser models, however, were impressive enough, and a 596cc Squirrel with 30bhp would do around 85mph, with a character all its own.

Suzuki T20 Super Six

Although there were a few six-cylinder race bikes on the scene by 1966, the name of that year's new Suzuki launch, the Super Six, didn't relate to the number of cylinders but to the number of gears, which in itself was a real rarity.

It was Suzuki's sportiest road bike to date, and although it was still only a small-capacity machine it soon built a big reputation. It looked good and matched those looks with both performance and handling. It was powered by an air-cooled, parallel-twin, two-stroke engine of 247cc, which had Posi-Force pressure lubrication and an excellent output of 29bhp.

In a bike which weighed only just over 300lb, and with the advantage of that six-speed gearbox, it had a claimed top speed of 100mph, and would get pretty close to it with a following wind and rider tucked down behind the high

BIKE FACT   First Built 1966

Six gears were a rarity in 1966, but that was only part of the Super Six's advanced specification.

handlebars. The Super Six boasted sharp
handling via externally-sprung front forks and
conventional rear swing arms mounted on what
was Suzuki's first-ever twin-tube cradle frame.
The bike was stopped by generously sized and
quite effective front and rear drum brakes. Until
Suzuki moved on and up into the big-capacity
market this was without a doubt their most
spectacular motorcycle.

Suzuki GT750

Suzuki didn't build their first motorcycle until 1952. By 1962 the company had won its first world title, in the 50cc class. Over the next decade and a half Suzuki worked their way up through the racing classes, via 125cc and 250cc to consolidate their racing successes with multiple 500cc world title wins in the early and mid-1970s. Alongside the racing successes, Suzuki also relentlessly built their road bike side.

In 1971 they joined the Japanese superbike battle that had been begun by the Honda CB750 in 1969. The two were very different bikes. The Honda was an air-cooled four-cylinder four-stroke, while the Suzuki had a similar capacity at 738cc, it was water-cooled, had three-cylinders and was a two-stroke. It famously became nicknamed 'the Kettle' for the polished jackets around the cylinders of its transverse engine. Far

BIKE FACT   First Built 1971
Suzuki's quiet and mild-mannered two-stroke triple had big roadgoing performance, and a serious racing role.

from being a two-stroke screamer, it was a much milder package, a big and fairly heavy sports tourer with flawed high-speed handling but good long-distance comfort and smooth power delivery through its five-speed gearbox. For a Suzuki two-stroke triple it was surprisingly docile, even quite quiet through its three-into-four exhausts and big twin silencers. With its final, 1975 upgrade it delivered 70bhp, and this with real flexibility rather than high-rev temperament. This made the GT750 fast enough for most at 120mph, but with a very gentle heart.

Suzuki RE5

Hamstrung by excessive fuel consumption and emissions worries, the rotary engine developed by Dr Felix Wankel turned into one of motoring's great lost causes, but not before both two- and four-wheeled worlds had given it a fair try. On two wheels, without ignoring the efforts and successes of Norton, it was Suzuki who made the biggest production impact, with its RE5, launched in 1974. Unlike the twin-rotor Nortons, the RE5 had a water-cooled single-rotor Wankel engine of a nominal 497cc capacity, mounted across the frame. 'Nominal' because there remained a question

BIKE FACT   First Built 1974

With its RE5, Suzuki made big efforts to make rotary power work with two wheels.

mark over how to measure the capacity and even in some opinions how to define the engine's cycle, somewhere between a two-stroke and a four-stroke, given the rotary's equivalent of piston-ported valving, the RE5's separate two-stroke oil feed, and the firing pattern of the three-sided rotor. Either way, the RE5 was a bulky, weighty tourer, with adequate rather than special ride and handling. Its 62bhp offered a maximum of only around 110mph, but with the fringe benefits of the rotary's smoothness and flexibility in a bike whose styling was as unconventional as its choice of power unit.

Suzuki Katana 1100

The Katana 1100 was named after a Samurai warrior's ceremonial sword, and the sharpest first impression of this super-modern superbike was its extraordinary styling, with angular lines in the tall tank, running through seat and side mouldings and carrying forwards through a mini-fairing which had an air-intake below and the rectangular headlamp and vestigial screen above. The look was absolutely original, and before long widely imitated in various adaptations, and the Katana still looks pretty spectacular even today.

It was launched in 1982 and the styling (by the not very Japanese Jan Fellstrom) was amply backed up by the Katana's performance potential. Its twin-cam 16-valve transverse four was air-cooled, with four carburettors, driven through a five-speed gearbox and chain final drive, and produced a hefty 111bhp. However, what most

BIKE FACT   First Built 1982

The Katana's radical styling and high performance were as sharp as the sword after which the bike was named.

testers noted was the abundance of low-speed torque when compared with some other four-valve fours. Admittedly it was quite heavy, at over 550lb, but that great flexibility and top-end power saw it up to more than 135mph, with excellent handling from a well-developed but conventional frame, all of which was a combination to get the Katana noticed even if its wild looks hadn't already.

Suzuki GSX-R750

Launched in 1985, the GSX-R750 was widely heralded as the first 'real' race replica, a bike that didn't just pretend to have race relations, but was genuinely derived, with very few changes, from the factory endurance racers. It wasn't even based on last year's model. In this case, the works racers were versions of the current GSX-R750 customer bikes. Yet it was a fully road-legal package that Suzuki dubbed their 'hyper sports' concept.

It was utterly uncompromising in the way it delivered its power (mostly at the top end of the rev range) and in its riding position. It also had fantastic aerodynamics and bodywork graphics, super-crisp handling and braking, and minimal ride comfort. Most of all, though, it had awesome performance. It was a real lightweight in literal terms, at less than 390lb, but the oil-cooled twin-cam 16-valve 749cc transverse four (which itself

BIKE FACT   First Built 1985

The light and powerful GSX was a big seller and started a popular fashion for 'race replicas'.

saved some 35lb weight when compared with its water-cooled cousin) produced around 102bhp, which helped to give the GSX-R750 a top speed of 145mph even in straight-out-of-the-box road bike form. Both on the road and on the track it was an enormous success, matching strong sales and a range-enhancing image with race wins and a big reputation.

Suzuki RG500

While making a big splash with their large-capacity four-strokes in the mid-1970s, Suzuki didn't desert their two-stroke roots. Building on two-stroke technology brought to Suzuki by former MZ racer Ernst Degner, the Japanese team won titles at 50, 125, 250 and, eventually, 500cc. The bike that finally brought multiple blue-riband 500 titles and several TT victories was the RG500, first raced in 1974 and starting its title haul in 1976. It was complex, but after early teething troubles it was also reliable. It had a water-cooled square-four engine, with disc valves, twin crankshafts and four individual cylinder barrels on a common crankcase. Originally it had oversquare dimensions, very little flexibility and 90bhp. Changed to exactly square dimensions and with other developments including making it slightly more compact, it gave 100bhp with better

BIKE FACT   First Built 1974

With multiple 500 championship and TT wins, the RG500 was one of Suzuki's most successful racers.

mid-range delivery and appropriately better
acceleration, later increased to 114bhp and finally
over 120. Top speed depended on gearing, but
more than 170mph was possible, and the RG500's
chassis – always excellent – also improved
continuously, eventually with composite frame
technology developed by the British Heron-
Suzuki race team, taking the RG500's winning
streak well into the 1980s with even lighter weight
and phenomenal stiffness.

Suzuki GSX-R1100

As night follows day, next step for the GSX-R750 was to get bigger, more powerful and faster. But unfortunately, far more troublesome. The development was the GSX-R1100, introduced in 1986. While retaining the keep-it-pure-and-keep-it-simple philosophy of the 750, the 1100 raised the stakes in almost every direction. Bore and stroke increases raised capacity of the twin-cam four to 1052cc and power to 125bhp, for a top speed of 155mph, made all the better by improved mid-range flexibility but with little change to the 750's attributes of light weight and racetrack handling. That was the good news; the bad news followed in 1989, when the GSX-1100R was further modified, but not further improved. Capacity increased again, to 1127cc, and power went up to 141bhp, which took top speed beyond 160mph, with fantastic urge at almost any speed.

BIKE FACT   First Built 1986

Suzuki grew the GSX-R750 into the superb R1100, but spoiled the plot when they tried to improve the recipe.

But a new chassis undid much of the good work, being slightly heavier and less road-user-friendly. With a shorter wheelbase and suspension geometry changes it was a good track bike and a nervous road bike, and although several new variants in the 1990s tried to repair the damage, they never really restored the handling qualities of the original.

Suzuki GSX1300R Hayabusa

In 1999, thirty years after Honda had created the superbike genre with the CB750F, roadgoing motorcycles passed a milestone that even five years ago seemed like pure fantasy, when the Suzuki GSX1300R Hayabusa posted a top speed of more than 200mph. This was completely new territory, unexplored even by Grand Prix racers until 1993, but now genuinely attainable. The secret is a mixture of big power and superb, low-drag aerodynamics. The Hayabusa has a twin-spar aluminium frame and box-section swinging arm, inverted forks and rear monoshock, triple discs, and special radial tyres on 17-inch wheels. It is lighter than most, at less than 475lb, and

BIKE FACT   First Built 1999

Big power and low aerodynamic drag helped the Hayabusa to break the 200mph barrier.

handles and stops impeccably, but the headline
news is in a straight line. Power is from a short-
stroke 1298cc in-line four, with twin cams, 16
valves, injection and electronic management. It
uses ram-fed intakes and four-into-two-into-one
exhaust. It produces 173bhp, and the other
element in achieving the double ton is that
exceptional streamlining, which combines a low
drag coefficient with a low frontal area to allow
the power to do its job at the very top end – and
finally to break that 200mph barrier.

Triumph Bonneville

In 1956 Johnny Allen rode a Triumph-powered streamliner across the Bonneville Salt Flats at 214mph and gave Triumph a name for their most sporty bike, unveiled in 1959. The T120 Bonneville started a long line, and developed from the T110 Tiger which had been the basis of Allen's record-breaker. The T120 had a 649cc version of Triumph's long-serving pushrod parallel twin, whose basics dated back to the mid-1930s but which was still one of the British industry's most respected engines. The Bonneville added twin carburettors, a stronger crankshaft and enough tuning to deliver 46bhp. The original had pre-unit four-speed gearbox (until 1963) and a single-tube frame (replaced by a twin-tube type in 1960). Looks improved too, with the original heavy-handed styling giving way to a much leaner line which better matched the Bonneville's

BIKE FACT   First Built 1959
The Bonneville not only looked great, it also won races, including the Isle of Man Production TT.

110mph performance. The handling never did quite, but it improved with the second version of the twin-tube frame in 1972, while capacity was increased to 744cc and power to 49bhp in the 1973 T140, although more weight meant no more top speed. It was enough, though, to make the Bonneville a race winner and a big seller, but not to survive the company's financial woes.

Triumph Trident

The story of the Triumph Trident, launched in 1968 as first cousin to the BSA Rocket 3, was in a way the story of the difference between the British and Japanese motorcycle industries in that crucial period when the superbike was being created and the industry was being realigned. It's history that the British industry was the loser, and fact that much of its problem was complacency. It's also true that in the last days of the big British sports bike and the early days of the Japanese superbike, the Japanese had the engines but the Brits had the frames and the handling. The Trident wasn't a bad example. Its air-cooled transverse three-cylinder engine was in effect one and a half traditional Triumph twins, giving 740cc and 58bhp. So the power didn't match the forthcoming Honda CB750, but in the lighter Triumph the power-to-weight ratio was very close

BIKE FACT   First Built 1968
The Trident's one and a half Triumph twins and fine handling couldn't stem the Japanese superbike tide.

behind, and the handling was widely
acknowledged to be well ahead of the first super-
Honda, so in some ways the 120mph Trident was
a surprisingly competitive proposition. But the
fact was, this was as far as this generation of
British bikes was going, and the Japanese
steamroller was only just starting.

Triumph Trophy 1200

The skin-of-the-teeth survival of the Triumph name after the final incarnation of the original company in 1983 and its rehabilitation through a difficult run-up to a production relaunch in the early 1990s is a minor miracle. The fact that when the famous name returned it did so with some genuinely excellent and exciting machines is perhaps an even bigger miracle.

The designs for the all new bikes were modern, both in styling and in technology terms, and the resulting products were quick, well built and suddenly very desirable. The original six-bike range was extremely cleverly designed around a 'modular' engine system, allowing closely related water-cooled twin-cam three- and four-cylinder engines to share many major components and thereby save large amounts of design and manufacturing cost.

BIKE FACT   First Built 1991

That Triumph survived was a surprise, that it revived was a miracle; the Trophy was both.

They were also good engines, smooth and strong, in very effective frames. The latter were best described as stiff steel 'backbones', carrying bought-in suspension and triple-disc brake components – mainly from Japan. The range-topping Trophy 1200 was a handsomely-faired sports bike with an 1180cc 16-valve four, delivering 125bhp through a six-speed gearbox, for a maximum of 150mph. Some 25 years after Japan had invented the super-sports bike, Britain had finally built a worthy rival.

Triumph T509 Speed Triple

The three-cylinder prong of Triumph's 1990s fightback was another superb bike, and while the bigger four-cylinder Triumphs ably looked after the top end of the market, the new triples recreated a long-lost reputation for big performance with crisp and agile handling from a mid-sized sports machine.

The star of the range was the T509 Speed Triple (reprising the famous name of the original Speed Twin), which was launched in 1997. The very compact, modular engine design gave the twin-cam three-cylinder a capacity of 885cc and a dozen valves, with triple carbs and three-into-two exhausts helping it up to a very respectable 97bhp, with a sweet nature and a lovely mechanical sound. It was uncompromisingly a sports bike, with hump-backed tank and clip-on style bars, without fairings or frills, but with big

BIKE FACT   First Built 1997

A superb modular engine gave Triumph the ability to create three-cylinder gems like the T509 Triple.

radial tyres on three-spoke alloy wheels
emphasising the power. It had larger, perforated
triple-disc brakes, and adjustable suspension, in a
package weighing just over 450lb. It looked
especially purposeful in all-black livery, including
the wheels, the exhausts and even the engine and
gearbox casings. Best of all, as far as the company
was concerned, it began to sell as well as it looked
and performed.

Van Veen OCR1000

It was odd that a man who created a series of
world championship-winning 50cc racers should
possibly be better remembered for producing a
massive rotary-engined superbike. He was a
Dutchman, Henk van Veen, and the 50cc racers
were the German Kreidlers, which he ran on
behalf of the works in the early 1970s, taking
several world titles with the bikes.

The big bike bore his own name. It was the
Van Veen, and it appeared in 1972, intended as
a luxurious, comfortable and refined fast tourer,
for people who wanted something different and
who didn't mind paying for it. Because when it
was produced it was one of the most expensive
bikes in the world. The first versions were
powered by a car-derived Mazda rotary engine,
but by 1974 there was a new model, the
OCR1000, with a new engine, developed for

BIKE FACT   First Built 1972

When too much wasn't quite enough, Van Veen built
some of the biggest and heaviest bikes in the world.

Van Veen by the Citroën offshoot company
Comotor. It was a twin-rotor unit, with a capacity
of 996cc and producing 100bhp. The extremely
heavy, full-bodied, shaft-driven bike needed the
power, but big torque and smoothness meant a
four-speed gearbox was enough, and claimed top
speed was 150mph, with smooth acceleration
from little more than walking pace. But, of
course, it was too different to last.

Velocette Venom Thruxton

Bonneville, Daytona, Ulster, Monza, Le Mans. The history of fast bikes is dotted with references both to race wins and record attempts. In Velocette's case the name wasn't quite as glamorous perhaps, but the machine that carried it was one of the greatest. It was the Venom Thruxton, launched in 1965, named for the circuit near Andover, Hampshire, where Velocette had won the famous 500-mile production race in 1964. That joined a long list of Junior TT wins and 350 world championships and speed records, all featuring Velocette's favoured four-stroke singles. The Thruxton was another, a café racer clone of the 499cc Venom, built as a replica of the 1964 500-mile winner and king of the 500 singles in the mid-1960s. Its pushrod overhead-valve vertical single, with precisely square bore and stroke dimensions, had

---

BIKE FACT   First Built 1965

The Thruxton proved its pedigree by taking first and second places in the first production TT in 1967.

a big-valve head, modified valvegear and huge
Amal racing carburettor, producing a strong
but infamously temperamental 40bhp, delivered –
sometimes none too smoothly – through a four-
speed gearbox. The road bike would hit as much
as 105mph, the TT-winning racer rather more,
and with its racing-style seat, clip-on bars, alloy-
rimmed wheels and air-scooped front drum
brake, the Thruxton looked the part, and more
than delivered.

Vincent Black Shadow

From the mid-1930s to the early 1950s, the 500 and 1000cc Vincents were the world's fastest standard production motorcycles. They were true thoroughbreds, full of highly individual design details, exquisite build quality and muscular good looks. The company grew out of the collapsed HRD, rebuilt in 1928 by Philip Vincent, joined in 1933 by the brilliant designer Phil Irving. They never made bikes in great quantities, but they built huge reputations with their Comets, Rapides, Black Lightnings – and the ultimate 1000 vee-twin, the Black Shadow. The first twin was created in 1936 by combining two 499 Comet singles in a 47-degree vee, for the superfast but often troublesome Rapide. That was improved

BIKE FACT   First Built 1948
For three decades Vincent built the world's fastest
production bikes, gaining a huge reputation.

after World War II in the Series B, its redesigned 50-degree twin used as a load-carrying part of the 'frameless' backbone structure, allowing a lighter, stiffer, shorter-wheelbase package. The sporty Black Shadow Series C, introduced in 1949, made fine use of Vincent's complex but effective Girdraulic front and swing-frame rear suspension and dual drum brakes on each wheel, with a potent 55bhp from its all-black-finished engine producing a maximum of more than 120mph – or in tuned, record-breaking trim, over 150mph.

Yamaha XS1100

It took a while for Yamaha truly to get into the big league of superbike performance, and when they did take the plunge they did it with a subtle difference of emphasis.

In 1978 they launched the XS1100, and while it had the power and performance closely to match Japanese rivals like the Honda CBX, the Suzuki GS1000 and the Kawasaki Z1, it had a character of its own, which was much more superfast long-distance tourer than outright sports bike. It had shaft drive, electric starter, halogen headlamp, self-cancelling indicators, and a big, touring-range fuel tank. It was big and comfortable, with a wide, well-padded seat and adjustable damping front and rear, although that didn't mean you threw it around. It was heavy and apparently lazy, but the laziness was deceptive. The air-cooled twin-cam, eight-valve

---

BIKE FACT   First Built 1978

Shaft drive and an emphasis on ride comfort made the XS1100 a subtly different kind of 1970s superbike.

four-stroke four, with four carburettors,
developed 95bhp, and although the XS1100
weighed more than 560lb that gave a top speed of
almost 135mph. The big Yamaha's real forte,
though, was its remarkable smoothness and
massive flexibility. From walking pace to
maximum, in any of its five gears, it responded
instantly, strongly and smoothly – a slow burn but
a very big punch.

Yamaha RD500LC

Others were quick to follow, but Yamaha were first to produce that modern incarnation of the old café racer, the road-replica two-stroke GP racer. They did it in 1984, with the RD500LC, first cousin to the racing RD500 and the already established RD350LC. Like the 350, the RD500LC was close to the specification of the racing model that inspired it. And to the character. It started as a strictly limited edition, and many early customers took it straight back to the track. They could, because the RD500LC was light and compact as well as powerful and fast. Race-ready handling came from an aluminium tube frame with rear monoshock located under the engine for the tightest packaging. Brakes were big and powerful triple discs, the gearbox had six closely-spaced ratios and power was plentiful. It came from a liquid-cooled, 499cc, twin-crank,

---

BIKE FACT   First Built 1984

The RD500LC was a production version of Yamaha's classic four-cylinder two-stroke 500 race winners.

reed-valved, 50-degree vee-four, with Yamaha's 'power-valve' variable-exhaust-port timing. It had all the pedigree of what were then the world's most successful two-stroke race-engine builders, and produced 90bhp, mostly very close to the top of the rev range, for a maximum of at least 140mph and real race-bike single-mindedness.

Yamaha FJ1100

As most of the early four-stroke big-bangers
demonstrated, power and performance without
poise was a very compromised package, and there
was no escaping the fact that most of the early
Japanese 1000-plus bikes were bigger on speed
than on handling. The Yamaha FJ1100 addressed
the problem with a well-balanced and fine-
handling chassis that took the fear if not the
excitement out of the big performance. The gain
was more about weight distribution, keeping the
weight as low as possible and the frame as stiff as
possible, than about weight saving. So the top
end of the engine was sandwiched between two
box-section steel tubes above a wide lower cradle.
Yamaha dubbed it their lateral frame concept,
and it became a widely copied layout. Power, an
enormously impressive 125bhp, came from a
1097cc air-cooled, twin-cam, transverse four,

BIKE FACT   First Built 1984

The FJ1100 added superb handling to ample power
for a superb overall package.

which gave a top speed of more than 150mph. The big gain, though, was, as intended, in usable performance through friendly handling. The ultra-stiff steering-head location, low centre of gravity and unusually small wheels gave the FJ1100 unrivalled agility alongside its contemporaries, and a deserved reputation as a big bike that really broke the mould.

Yamaha V-Max

The V-Max, launched in 1984 and destined for a very long production life, had a very specific agenda. It didn't want to be the fastest bike on the block, just the fastest-accelerating – a street dragster, if you like, rather than a street racer. Its looks told the story. A low-rider seating position, high bars, long front fork rake, massively chunky rear tyre and very little concern for high-speed aerodynamics. Not that it wasn't pretty quick: almost 140mph maximum was good stuff for what looked like a Japanese Harley with lots of custom touches including polished alloy dish wheels, giant megaphone-shaped exhausts and dramatic silver airscoops (although they were not functional). The liquid-cooled vee-twin had a capacity of 1198cc and four downdraught carburettors under the dummy tank (the real one is under the seat). The engine delivered 138bhp,

BIKE FACT   First Built 1984
Given it's hot-rod demeanour, it's not surprising the V-Max is very popular with custom-bike builders.

and the five-speed shaft-drive transmission was geared to use all its considerable torque for just one purpose, acceleration. As launched, the V-Max, simply, was the fastest-accelerating production road bike in the world, capable of sub 10.5-second standing quarters and much lower after popular after-market tweaking. And to the V-Max enthusiast, that feeling of neck snapping acceleration was what really mattered.

Yamaha FZR 750R

For the superbike aficionado, World Superbike racing has many attractions: top-quality racing and the chance for marque patriotism are two, but there's an important third. To qualify for the racing ranks, manufacturers have to comply with technical regulations, and also fulfil a minimum production requirement related to the number of 'ordinary' production bikes they build in a year.

In the late 1980s, for the biggest that meant producing a run of a thousand machines. That was far too many to sell purely as customer racing bikes, hence the vogue for road-legal World Superbikes. Yamaha's 1989 offering took the form of the FZR 750R. Its frame is made of a light, super-stiff aluminium Deltabox, with telescopic front and race-type rear monoshock, for race-ready handling. Brakes are triple discs, and the four-stroke engine is a 749cc liquid-

---

BIKE FACT   First Built 1989

The FZR 750R was created in order to meet the world superbike homologation rules.

cooled, twin-cam, in-line four, with five valves per cylinder, four carburettors, big valves, an exceptionally short stroke and Yamaha's EXUP variable-exhaust geometry. The latter is designed to broaden the torque spread for such a highly-tuned engine, and does so pretty effectively, giving usable mid-range as well as a maximum of 120bhp. This results in the 415lb bike doing a maximum speed of more than 160mph.

Yamaha FZR 1000 EXUP

EXUP? That is the shorthand for Yamaha's power-valve exhaust technology, a system designed to reconcile the apparently incompatible aims of maximum top-end power with acceptable low- to mid-range flexibility in a highly-tuned four-stroke engine. The basis is to vary the effective length of the exhaust tract depending on engine speed, which EXUP achieved by an electronically-controlled rotary valve within the exhaust system. It was added to the FZR 1000 in 1989, when capacity was also increased from 989 to 1002cc, and the rest of the FZR 1000's engine technology is more conventional – a liquid-cooled twin-cam in-line four with five valves per cylinder, producing

BIKE FACT   First Built 1989
Yamaha's EXUP – power-valve exhaust technology – combines power with flexibility.

140bhp and, as desired, a very usable mid-range spread. Maximum speed was close to 170mph and many thought that the FZR 1000 EXUP was among the best of the big Japanese sports bikes of the late 1980s and early 1990s. Treated with appropriate respect, it handled too. With a low-centre-of-gravity chassis, closely related to the Genesis racing bike's Deltabox layout, plus large-diameter front forks, triple-disc brakes with floating discs, and a fairly short wheelbase, it had superb responses, if not much ride comfort.

Yamaha YZF1000-R1

By the late 1990s, superbike enthusiasts increasingly expected something very close to race bike performance for the road, and the YZF1000-R1 introduced another Grand Prix bike trick to the road, with an extra-long rear swing-arm suspension layout that was said to help traction out of corners, while allowing the wheelbase and overall length to be kept short and sporty. That becomes important when, come the 1999 version, you are delivering a claimed 150bhp at the flywheel, and offering a top speed of more than 175mph, with a world-class quarter-mile time of just 10.3 seconds at a terminal speed of 133mph. Apparently the latest traction tweak worked for the handling too, and

BIKE FACT   First Built 1998
With power and performance continuing their climb, Yamaha looked to handling with the YZF1000-R1.

at least one tester reckoned the 1-litre R1 'steered and cornered better than any 600 or 750'. This was now the state of the art. The YZF1000-R1 had a 998cc liquid-cooled, four-stroke in-line four, and weighing less than 400lb it was certainly one of the lightest packages in its capacity class, with knock-on benefits to performance, handling, braking and agility – all earning the YZF1000-R1 a reputation as the benchmark sports bike of its late-1990s generation.

Glossary

ABS: Antilock Braking
System: sensors in the brakes
sense impending skidding and
prevent it, allowing greater
control of the vehicle.

belt drive: rear wheel driven
by a belt as opposed to a
chain, used extensively on
modern Harleys.

bhp: 'brake horsepower',
measurement of the power
output of an engine,
measured by a brake applied
to the drive shaft.

bore: the diameter of the
cylinder.

café racer: pared-down bike
style that grew out of riders
meeting at and racing
between cafés in the 1950s.
Pages 7 & 43 are examples.

calipers: part of disc-brake
mechanism that forces the
brake pads against the
revolving brake disc.

cam/camshaft: cams are
irregularly-shaped metal lobes
on the camshaft which rotate
and so govern the opening
and closing of the inlet and
exhaust valves.

capacity: the volume of the
engine's cylinders. Larger
capacity allows more power.
Measured in litres or cubic
centimetres (cc), or cubic
inches (cu in) in the USA.

carburettor: mixes and
controls the delivery of fuel
and air to the cylinders.

chain drive: rear wheel is
driven by a chain.

clip-on (style) bars: short
drop bars that attach directly
to the top of the forks.

compression: the process that
fuel in the cylinder undergoes
before ignition, which
increases its explosive energy.
Caused by the piston. Higher

compression gives more power but less flexibility.

crankshaft: the shaft at the bottom of the engine driven by the pistons.

cylinder: the cylinder houses the piston and is where combustion takes place.

damper: see *shock absorber*.

desmodromic valvegear: cam-driven closing mechanisms that eliminate the need for valve springs, used extensively in Ducati engines.

disc brake: mechanism that uses pads to grip a revolving disc attached to the wheel to slow it. Generally more efficient than older-style drum brakes.

drag coefficient: a measure of air resistance or 'drag'.

drum brake: mechanism that forces a friction pad attached to a 'shoe' outwards against a drum-like housing attached to the revolving wheel.

emissions: the components of exhaust gases harmful to the environment.

fairing: bodywork that wraps around the front of the bike.

finning: the thin metal fins that surround the engine block and air-cool the engine.

forks: the two shafts between which the front wheel sits.

Formula 1: possibly the highest class of bike racing, the other contender being World Superbike.

four: four-cylinder engine.

four-stroke: see *two-stroke*.

frame: the chassis around which the bike is built.

fuel injection: fuel is injected directly into the cylinder rather than being mixed with air via a carburettor.

girder forks: solid rather than telescopic forks.

homologation: building a limited number of bikes to qualify as eligible to compete in a 'production' racing class.

horsepower: measure of the engine's power output.

monocoque: one-piece body construction with no separate frame.

monoshock: suspension set-up using single, as opposed to dual, shock absorbers.

overhead cam: camshaft sitting above the valves, allowing higher revving and more performance than if it is placed low in the engine.

pot: nickname for cylinder.

production bike: a 'normal' bike available to the general public, as opposed to racing

bikes or limited-run 'specials'.

pushrod: rod transmitting the action of the cams to the valves.

rear end: rear of the bike's frame.

reed valves: flap-like high-performance inlet valves for two-stroke engines.

rocker-covers: the housings covering the valve mechanisms at the top of the engine block.

shaft drive: the rear wheel is driven by a shaft, much like a car.

shock absorber: suspension component that controls the bike's ride.

stressed element: component of the bike, such as the engine, that also functions as part of the bike's frame.

stroke: the length of the piston's travel.

stroker: a nickname for a two-stroke bike.

sump: pan at the bottom of the engine that holds oil for lubrication. In a 'dry sump' oil is circulated by high-pressure pumps rather than being held in a 'pool'.

supercharger: pump driven off the engine that forces fuel and air into the engine under pressure, so allowing more power.

swinging-arm suspension: wheel suspended by an arm assembly hinged at the frame.

torque: measure of the turning power produced by the engine.

turbocharger: pump boosting the pressure at which fuel is delivered to the engine. The pump is powered by the engine's own exhaust gases, this cycle often resulting in a 'lag' before the performance effect from the turbo is felt.

triple: three-cylinder engine.

twin: two-cylinder engine.

two or four-stroke (engine): the four-stroke cycle comprises separate movements of the piston for Induction, Compression, Power and Exhaust. In the two-stroke engine the cycle is combined into an Induction and Compression stroke and Power and Exhaust stroke.

valve: allows the fuel mixture into the cylinder and the exhaust out. High-performance engines often have multi-valves per cylinder to increase the flow.

wheelbase: the distance between the wheels of the bike.

works-prepared: racing bike prepared by the manufacturer rather than a private racing team.

Pictures

The publishers would like to thank the following for their kind courtesy in supplying images and for giving permissions for their use in this book:

Aprilla Motorcyles, Peter Bell, Les Bensley, Bimota Motor S.p.A., BMW (GB) Ltd, Don Morley International Sports Photo Agency, Harley-Davidson United Kingdom, Jurgen Hecker, Honda Motorcycles, Kawasaki Motors (UK) Ltd, Laverda, Andrew Morland, Moto Cinelli, National Motor Museum, Suzuki Motorcycles, Suzuki Owners Club, Richard Taylor, Three Cross Motorcycles Ltd, Triumph Motorcycles Limited, Vincent HRD Owners Club, Yamaha Motorcycles.

COLLINS GEM
BABIES' names
a ? z
a mine of information

COLLINS GEM
BEER
a mine of information

COLLINS GEM
BIRDS
a mine of information

COLLINS GEM
CALORIE Counter
a mine of information

COLLINS GEM
FACT FILE
a mine of information

COLLINS GEM
FENG SHUI
a mine of information

COLLINS GEM
FLAGS
a mine of information

COLLINS GEM
Healthy EATING
a mine of information

COLLINS GEM
QUOTATIONS
a mine of information

COLLINS GEM
SAS Self-Defence
a mine of information

COLLINS GEM
SAS Survival Guide
a mine of information

COLLINS GEM
SEASHORE
a mine of information

COLLINS GEM
TREES
a mine of information

COLLINS GEM
Understanding DREAMS
a mine of information

COLLINS GEM
WILD flowers
a mine of information

COLLINS GEM
WINE Dictionary
a mine of information